CONTRIBUTORS AND CONSULTANTS

HALL BARTLETT, *Ed.D., Citizenship Education Project, Teachers College, Columbia University; Author*

WALT DISNEY, *Motion Picture and Television Producer*

EVELYN MILLIS DUVALL, *Ph.D., Author and Consultant on Family Life; Authority on Child Development*

EDNA E. EISEN, *Ph.D., Professor of Geography, Kent State University*

J. ALLEN HYNEK, *Ph.D., Associate Director, Smithsonian Astrophysical Observatory*

LELAND B. JACOBS, *Ph.D., Professor of Education, Teachers College, Columbia University*

ELEANOR M. JOHNSON, *M.A., Director of Elementary School Services, Graduate Division, Wesleyan University*

HERBERT A. LANDRY, *M.S.,Ph.D.,Director,Bureau of Educational Program Research and Statistics, New York City Public Schools*

MILTON LEVINE, *M.D.,Associate Professor of Pediatrics,New York Hospital*

WILLY LEY, *Professor of Science, Fairleigh Dickinson University; Rocket Expert and Author*

NORMAN LLOYD, *M.A., Teacher of Literature and Materials of Music, Juilliard School of Music*

LENOX R. LOHR, *M.E., D.Eng., D.Sc., President, Museum of Science and Industry, Chicago*

WILL C. MCKERN, *D.S., Former Director, Milwaukee Public Museum; Anthropologist*

RICHARD A. MARTIN, *B.S., Curator, N. W. Harris Public School Extension, Chicago Natural History Museum*

MAURICE PATE, *Executive Director, United Nations Children's Fund (UNICEF)*

NORMAN VINCENT PEALE, *D.D., LL.D., Litt.D., LH.D.; Minister, Marble Collegiate Church, New York; Author*

RUTHERFORD PLATT, *B.A., Member of Two North Pole Expeditions with Admiral MacMillan; Author of Nature Books*

ILLA PODENDORF, *M.S., Teacher of Science, University of Chicago Laboratory Schools; Author of Science Books*

MARY M. REED, *Ph.D.,Supervisor of Little Golden Books; Formerly of Teachers College, Columbia University*

JOHN R. SAUNDERS, *M.A., Chairman, Department of Public Instruction, American Museum of Natural History*

GLENN T. SEABORG, *Ph.D., LL.D., D.Sc., Chancellor and Professor of Chemistry, University of California, Berkeley; Associate Director, University of California Radiation Laboratory; Co-winner of Nobel Prize for Chemistry, 1951*

LOUIS SHORES, *Ph.D., Dean of the Library School, Florida State University; Author and Authority on Reference Materials*

NILA BANTON SMITH, *Ph.B., Ph.D., Professor of Education and Director of The Reading Institute, New York University*

BRYAN SWAN, *M.S., Teacher of Physical Science, University of Chicago Laboratory Schools; Author*

SAMUEL TERRIEN, *S.T.M., Th.D., Auburn Professor of the Old Testament, Union Theological Seminary*

JESSIE TODD, *M.A., Formerly of the Art Department, University of Chicago; Art Lecturer; Contributor to Art Magazines*

LLOYD B. URDAL, *Ph.D.,Assistant Professor,School of Education, State College of Washington*

JANE WERNER WATSON, *B.A., Editor and Author of More Than a Hundred Golden Books*

WILLIAM S. WEICHERT, *M.S., Supervisor of Science, Oakland (Calif.) Public Schools*

PAUL A. WITTY, *Ph.D., Professor of Education, Northwestern University; Specialist on Gifted Children*

STAFF

ROBERT D. BEZUCHA, *Project Director;* NORMAN F. GUESS, *Editorial Director;* R. JAMES ERTEL, *Managing Editor;* PAULINE NORTON, *Assistant Project Director;* ALICE F. MARTIN, *Associate Editor. Staff Editors:* GENEVIEVE CURLEY, JOAN FALK, HESTER GELB, RICHARD D. HARKINS.

THE GOLDEN BOOK ENCYCLOPEDIA

VOLUME XIV—SILK TO TEXTILES

In Sixteen Accurate, Fact-filled Volumes Dramatically Illustrated
with More Than 6,000 Color Pictures

THE ONLY ENCYCLOPEDIA FOR YOUNG GRADE-SCHOOL CHILDREN

ACCURATE AND AUTHORITATIVE

ENTERTAININGLY WRITTEN AND ILLUSTRATED TO
MAKE LEARNING AN ADVENTURE

by Bertha Morris Parker

Formerly of the Laboratory Schools, University of Chicago
Research Associate, Chicago Natural History Museum

GOLDEN PRESS · NEW YORK

Illustrations from GOLDEN BOOKS, published by Golden Press, Inc., New York, © 1949, 1951, 1952, 1953,
1954, 1955, 1956, 1957 by Golden Press, Inc.; from the Golden Stamp Book WILD LIFE WONDERS, ©
1958 by Golden Press, Inc.; from the Basic Science Education Series (Unitext), published by Row, Peterson
and Company, Evanston, Illinois, © 1941, 1942, 1943, 1947, 1952, 1957, 1959 by Row, Peterson and
Company; and from SPACE STATIONS, published by Guild Press, Inc., © 1958 by General Mills, Inc.

LIFE HISTORY OF THE SILKWORM MOTH

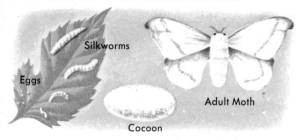

SILK Silkworms have been making silk for themselves for millions of years. These worms are the caterpillars, or larvas, of the silkworm moth. They use the silk they make for their cocoons. About 4,000 years ago the Chinese learned how to unravel cocoons made by silkworms and weave the silk into cloth.

Nobody is sure exactly when or how this great discovery was made. One story tells that one day in about 2700 B.C. a silkworm cocoon accidentally dropped into a cup of hot tea which a Chinese princess was drinking. When the princess tried to remove it, the cocoon unraveled and what she pulled out of her teacup was a long strand of silk thread.

Another story is that Hoang-ti, the emperor of China in 1700 B.C., became interested in silkworm cocoons. He told his young queen, Sing Li Chi, to find out whether the thread in the cocoons could be made useful. The queen, who was only 14 years old, set about raising and studying silkworms. Finally she learned how to unravel the silk and to weave it into cloth. The Chinese were so happy over Queen Sing Li Chi's discovery that they forever after called her the goddess of the silkworm.

For hundreds of years the Chinese made silk cloth and sold it to people all over Asia and Europe. They were, however, forbidden to tell how the cloth was made. But it was so beautiful that people everywhere were eager to learn the secret of making it. Gradually the information leaked out.

In the sixth century Justinian, the Roman emperor, learned the secret from two Persian monks who had been traveling in China. With the promise of a rich reward he persuaded them to go back to China and bring him some silkworm eggs. The monks returned with the eggs. They had smuggled them out of China by hiding them in a hollow bamboo cane. It is said that all the silk produced by Western countries since that time can be traced back to those eggs.

Silk-making is rather complicated. First the eggs are laid by the female silkworm moths on cards. Since the eggs are sticky, they remain attached to the cards. They hatch in about ten days into tiny wormlike larvas. The larvas, or silkworms, are then carefully examined. All sickly worms are destroyed. The healthy ones are spread out on trays and given mulberry leaves to eat. To the silk industry, raising healthy mulberry trees is just as important as raising healthy silkworms.

After about 25 days of continuous eating, the silkworms are ready to spin their silk cocoons. They are now fully grown. About one-fifth of their weight is silk. The silk is stored in two sacs, one on each side of the body. Both sacs are connected by means of tubes to an opening called the spinneret. This is located just below the

SILK AND ITS USES

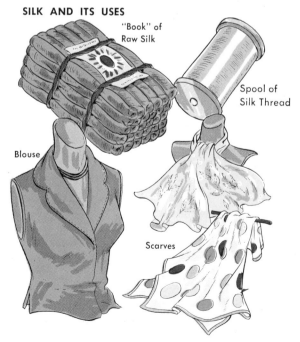

"Book" of Raw Silk

Spool of Silk Thread

Blouse

Scarves

mouth. The silk comes out of the worm's body as one thread. The silkworm fastens the end of the thread to a stick or some other support and then proceeds to wind the thread around its body. It winds the thread in a figure eight, so that the cocoon when finished is sometimes pinched in the middle like a peanut. The spinning is completed in about 24 hours.

Inside the cocoon the silkworm begins its remarkable change to a full-grown moth. Not all the silkworms are allowed to develop, however—only those that are needed for laying eggs. In crawling out of their cocoons the moths break the threads and make the cocoons useless for making thread for cloth. The moths that are allowed to come out of their cocoons live for a very short time. They fly about very little. They live only long enough to mate and to lay their eggs.

Most of the cocoons are placed in refrigerators to kill the silkworms inside. They are then placed in boiling water to soften the gum which holds the threads together. Special brushes are used to help clean the silk and to find the end of the thread. The silk in a cocoon is one long unbroken thread. When completely unwound it may be from 500 to 1,300 yards long. The threads from five or six cocoons are brought together and wound on a large reel, or spool, as one thread. When the threads from these cocoons have been completely unwound, threads from other cocoons are fastened to them. The joining is done so skillfully that it does not show. When the silk is taken from the reels, it is twisted into skeins. These are then made into large bundles called bales and are shipped to silk cloth manufacturers.

For hundreds of years silk cloth was prized as the most beautiful and most luxurious of all materials for clothing. It is still prized, although some people think that nylon and some of the other man-made fibers are more beautiful. (See BUTTERFLIES AND MOTHS; TEXTILES.)

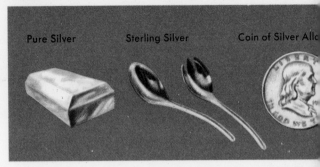

Pure Silver   Sterling Silver   Coin of Silver Allo

SILVER This valuable metal has been known and used by man since very early times. It was easy to discover because it is often found free in nature. It has only to be dug up and cleaned. Sometimes, however, silver is found in ores, where it is joined with other materials in what scientists call compounds.

Pure silver is almost white and very shiny. It is one of the most beautiful of all metals. But it is quite soft. Long ago metalworkers learned how to make silver harder by mixing a small amount of some harder metal with it.

For many, many centuries silver has been used as money. Coins were being made of it in Asia Minor 25 centuries ago. Four hundred years ago so much silver was found in Joachimsthal, in Bohemia, that a mint was built there. One of the silver coins made was called a "Joachimsthaler." This name was shortened to "thaler." "Dollar" comes from "thaler." The use of silver in jewelry goes far back, too.

Navaho Silversmith

One of the important uses for silver today is for tableware. Some tableware is "sterling" silver. Sterling silver is about nine-tenths silver and one-tenth copper.

Many people who cannot afford to buy sterling silver tableware buy silver plate instead. This is tableware made of some cheaper metal and coated with silver.

Silver is the best conductor of electricity known. This means that electricity passes through silver more easily than through any other substance known. Silver is also the best-known conductor of heat.

If silver objects are left in the open, they soon tarnish. To make them look shiny again they have to be polished. Silver tarnishes because small amounts of sulfur compounds in the air join with the sil-

FORMS OF SILVER

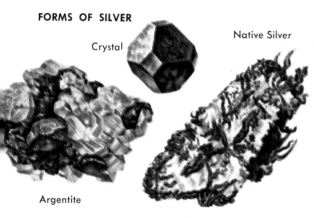

Crystal

Native Silver

Argentite

ver to make a dark-brown compound called silver sulfide. Eggs and some other foods also contain sulfur compounds which cause silverware to turn dark.

Some compounds of silver are easily affected by light. The light causes darker-colored compounds to form. For this reason silver compounds can be used for the taking of pictures. The film used in a camera has on it a coating of gelatin mixed with a silver compound.

Doctors often use silver in mending broken bones. Silver bands hold broken bones together. Silver plates take the place of skull bones that have been crushed. (See ELEMENTS; JEWELRY; METALS; MONEY; PHOTOGRAPHY; SULFUR.)

SKELETON A skeleton is useful to an animal in several ways. It makes a framework for the animal's body. It protects soft, delicate parts. A skeleton also helps the animal move, because muscles can be attached to it.

Some animals do not have a skeleton. A jellyfish, for example, does not. It does not need one. The water it lives in buoys it up. Its stinging cells protect it. And ocean currents move it along.

Most animals, however, have some kind of skeleton. It may be an inside skeleton, or it may be an outside skeleton.

The large group of animals called the jointed-legged animals have an outside skeleton. Spiders, crabs, lobsters, and all the insects are members of this group. Their skeleton is made of a material called chitin, which is very much like the material in our fingernails. It fits over the animal like a suit of armor. It is waterproof and thus helps keep the animal from becoming too wet or too dry. It has joints that make bending easy. Muscles are attached to the skeleton on the inside. One needs only to watch a beetle run to see how successful this kind of arrangement is.

Animals like the snail and clam also have an outside skeleton. Theirs, however, is not made of chitin but of lime. It is thick and heavy. The main purpose of such a skeleton is to protect the animal inside. Animals with this kind of skeleton move about slowly if at all.

All the large animals we know best have an inside skeleton. Their skeleton is made of bone. All animals with a bony skeleton are called vertebrates. A vertebrate's skeleton, even though it is on the inside, has a great deal to do with the animal's shape.

Some animals have both an inside and an outside skeleton. The turtles, for example, have an inside skeleton of bones and an outside skeleton that is made up of bony plates.

The human skeleton is made up of about 200 bones. When we are babies, our bones are mostly cartilage. Cartilage is the same as gristle. It is not hard and stiff like bone. As we grow, new cartilage is made, and most of the older cartilage changes to bone. A person does not stop adding cartilage till he is about 20 years old. When he stops adding cartilage, he stops growing. His skeleton is as big as it will ever be. (See BODY, HUMAN; BONES; INVERTEBRATES; VERTEBRATES.)

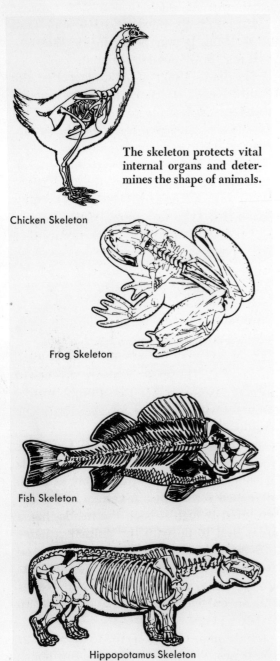

The skeleton protects vital internal organs and determines the shape of animals.

Chicken Skeleton

Frog Skeleton

Fish Skeleton

Hippopotamus Skeleton

SKIN Our skin separates each of us from the outside world. Through its nerves it sends to our brains many messages about what is going on around us. It tells us that the wind is blowing. It lets us know whether the day is hot or cold. It gives much information about the objects which we handle in our work or play. It tells us if something is rough or smooth, wet or dry, hard or soft.

Our skin forms a protective covering for the body. It helps protect the body from injury and helps keep germs from entering. It helps keep the body from drying out and from becoming too hot or too cold.

The skin is made up of two main layers. The outside layer is called the epidermis. Another name for it is cuticle. The part of this layer which is exposed to the air is made of dead cells which gradually rub off. In the other part of the layer new cells are made to replace the dead cells.

Beneath the epidermis lies the dermis. It is sometimes called the true skin. This layer is much thicker than the epidermis. It is made mostly of tough fibers. In some animals this part of the skin is so strong that we use it for making leather. In the dermis there are many nerves. There are many blood vessels, too. Blood vessels are elastic. When the body is very warm, they become larger and fill very full of blood. Heat can then pass from the blood out into the air through the skin to cool the body. When the body is cold, the blood vessels remain small so that heat will not be lost rapidly from the body.

Sometimes when a person becomes embarrassed many of the tiny blood vessels in his face get larger. His face becomes red, and we say that he is blushing.

In the lower part of the dermis there is a layer made mostly of fat cells. This layer of fat acts as an insulator. In the winter it helps keep heat inside the body. In summer it helps keep heat out. In whales this layer of fat is called blubber. It protects the whale against the cold ocean water.

Hairs, oil glands, and sweat glands run outward from the dermis. Attached to each hair there are tiny muscles. Sometimes when we are cold these muscles contract and make many tiny bumps, or goose pimples, on our skin.

The oil glands pour oil out on the hair and skin to help keep them in good condition. Brushing our hair helps these glands do their work.

The sweat glands pour water out on the skin. This water is called sweat or perspiration. When the water evaporates, the skin and the rest of the body become cooler. On a very hot day the body may lose in sweat two or three quarts of water.

In the skin there are some cells that contain a colored material called pigment. When only a little pigment is present, the skin is very light in color. Dark skin has more pigment. Strong sunlight may make the skin produce more pigment. Suntan soon disappears, however, if we stay out of the sunshine. (See BIOLOGY; BLOOD; BODY, HUMAN; CELL; FRECKLES; HEALTH; VITAMINS.)

SKIN DIVING The underwater sport called skin diving is one of the fastest-growing sports in the United States. It got its start shortly after World War II, and by 1958 there were about 5,000,000 followers of the sport.

Skin divers do their diving without the protection of heavy, deep-sea diving suits. Most of them, however, wear face masks and equipment that permits them to breathe under water.

Some skin divers catch fish with spear guns or knives. Others use special underwater cameras to take pictures of fish and of beautiful underwater scenery. Still others look for sea caves and shipwrecks.

Skin diving has its dangers. One diver was towed a mile out to sea by a shark he had wounded. He was finally rescued by yachtsmen. (See DEEP-SEA EXPLORING; DIVING; SWIMMING.)

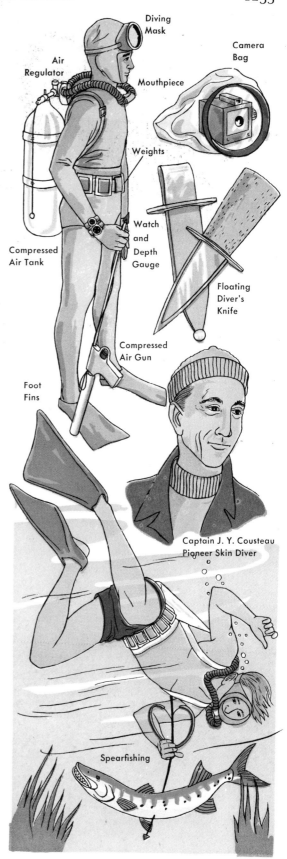

Diving Mask

Camera Bag

Air Regulator

Mouthpiece

Weights

Compressed Air Tank

Watch and Depth Gauge

Floating Diver's Knife

Compressed Air Gun

Foot Fins

Captain J. Y. Cousteau Pioneer Skin Diver

Spearfishing

Striped Skunk

SKUNK The skunk has a worse reputation than it deserves. Calling a person who has done something very wrong a skunk is not being fair to this animal. The skunk gets its bad reputation by its way of "answering back." When it is disturbed, it shoots out a liquid that has a very bad odor. The liquid comes from two scent glands just under the skunk's tail. Of course, shooting out the liquid is the animal's way of protecting itself.

Farmers do not like skunks because they sometimes kill chickens. But skunks pay for the chickens they eat by eating many mice and harmful insects.

Skunks are quite pretty with their black and white fur. And they are friendly animals. They seem to like to be near people. Often in the country a mother skunk makes a nest under the porch of a house when she is going to have her babies. Little skunks make good pets. They do not send out the bad-smelling liquid unless they are bothered. But to play safe it is wise to have a veterinarian remove the scent glands from a pet skunk.

Skunk's Footprints

Scent Gland

Spotted Skunks

Skunks are found all over North America. They live in woods, usually near the edges. Full-grown skunks are about the size of large cats. Sometimes they are called "wood pussies." They do their hunting at night. Unfortunately they have not learned that automobiles are dangerous. Many skunks are killed on roads. Hunters kill many others for their fur. (See FURS.)

SKY On a clear day the sky looks like a blue bowl turned upside down over the earth. People of long ago thought that it was a big bowl. The stars they saw at night they thought were holes, or windows, in the bowl. Some bright light from above the sky, they said, shone down through these windows.

Now we know that the sky is not like a bowl at all. It is not solid like a bowl. When we look up at the sky we are simply looking out into space.

The sky looks blue because of the air. The air around the earth scatters the sunlight that shines through it. Blue is one of the colors in sunlight. The air scatters the sunlight in such a way that we see blue rather than any of the other colors. If we could go up above the air, the sky would look black instead of blue.

Spotted Skunks

The air scatters light from the moon and the stars just as it does sunlight. There is blue in moonlight and starlight, too, but neither one is bright enough to give a very blue look to the night sky.

SKYSCRAPERS A skyscraper is a very tall building. Skyscrapers got their name because they look as if they were tall enough to touch the sky. "Skyscraper" is an American word, and most of the skyscrapers in the world are found in North and South America.

There is no point in having a skyscraper in a small town or city where there is plenty of room for buildings. Skyscrapers are built only in large cities where there is no room to spare.

Skyscrapers all have a skeleton of steel. The steel skeleton supports the tremendous weight of the building. Before men learned to build steel frameworks, big buildings had to have very thick walls, for the weight of the whole building rested on the walls. The walls had to be thicker at the bottom than at the top. In a skyscraper the outside walls are just the covering shell of the building. They do not have to be thicker near the ground. The walls of the lower stories do not even hold up the walls of the upper stories. The 20th or 30th story can be walled in before the first story, if the builder likes.

The steel skeleton of a skyscraper has to be very strong for more than one reason. It has to hold up the weight of the building. Besides, it has to be able to stand the force of the wind. The force of even an ordinary wind is very great against a tall building.

There is always a part of a skyscraper that no one ever sees. Much of such a big building is below the ground. A tall building has to be built with very solid foundations. The best plan is to sink them all the way down to solid rock—bedrock, it is called.

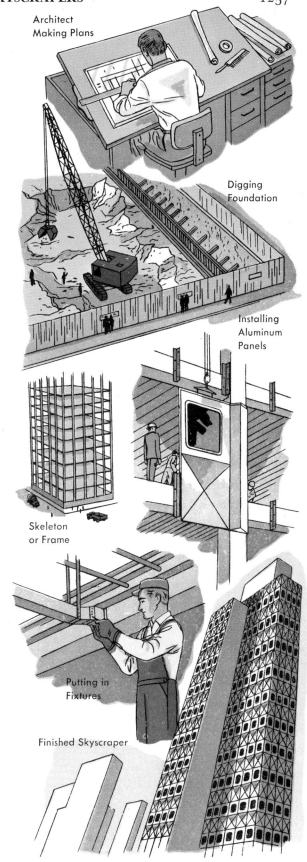

Architect Making Plans

Digging Foundation

Installing Aluminum Panels

Skeleton or Frame

Putting in Fixtures

Finished Skyscraper

The first building called a skyscraper was the Home Insurance Building, built in Chicago in 1885. It was 10 stories tall. The first giant skyscraper was the 60-story Woolworth Building in New York City. It was built in 1913.

The tallest skyscraper in the world is the Empire State Building in New York. This big office building soars into the air for 1472 feet—more than a quarter of a mile. It has 102 stories. The main part of the building is 85 stories. Above that there is a slender tower of 17 stories. In 1950 a 222-foot TV sending tower was added. The foundations rest on bedrock 55 feet below street level.

It took a tremendous amount of steel and stone to build this great building. The steel alone in it weighs more than 60,000 tons. The whole building weighs about 365,000 tons.

The Empire State Building is almost a city in itself. There is room in it for 80,000 people. If the elevator shafts were put one on top of the other they would reach up into the air for seven miles. There are enough electric wires in this building to reach nearly twice around the earth at the equator.

The men who worked at the top of the Empire State Building were working higher above the ground than any builders had ever worked before. One wonders whether any taller skyscraper will ever be built.

SKYWRITING The sky is the largest "blackboard" in the world. Thousands of messages are written on it each year. Most of the messages are advertisements. They generally tell the name of a product which an advertiser wants to sell.

Sometimes, however, skywriters write just for fun. Once two men played tick-tack-toe 10,000 feet up in the sky. Another time they flew over a schoolhouse and wrote "1 + 4 = 6" to tease the teachers and make the children laugh. But skywriting is usually too expensive to do just for

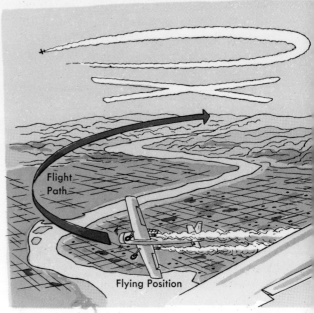

Flight Path

Flying Position

fun. Advertisers have to pay several thousand dollars for each message.

It takes a pilot about a year to become a good skywriter. He has to spend many hours practicing. He has to learn not only to write backwards, but also to write fast because the wind will soon blow his message away. Beginners follow a chart with the message written backwards on it. Experts write just by the "feel of it."

The writing is done with smoke made from a liquid carried in a tank. A pilot first tests the strength and direction of the wind. If the wind is not just right he moves higher or lower until he finds a suitable place. Then by pressing a trigger he sends some of the writing liquid into a section of the exhaust.

Here the heat from the hot gases of the engine change the liquid into very thick smoke which comes out of the plane in long white streams. The pilot does not write his letters up and down but lays them flat across the sky. They seem to be up and down, however, to people on the ground.

Each letter is about a mile long. A single word may stretch from ten to twenty miles. Long messages cannot be written because in about ten minutes the first letters usually begin to disappear.

Chemical Feed

Smoke Tube

Some letters are harder to write than others. Some pilots think that *S* is the hardest to write. Others think that *K* is. The word skywriters like best is "OXO," the name of a soup made in England. It can be written backwards, forwards, or upside down. It always spells "OXO."

Most skywriting is now done by two pilots working together. While one makes the upright of a *T*, the other crosses the *T*. The pilots do not bump into each other because the different parts of a letter do not actually touch. They are usually about 50 feet apart. When two pilots work together a message can be written faster and therefore read for a longer time.

The first words ever written in the sky were "Daily Mail," the name of an English newspaper. They were written on May 30, 1922, at Epsom Downs, a race track near London. The writer was Major J. C. Savage, the inventor of skywriting.

An American businessman, Allen J. Cameron, while visiting Europe, heard about this new kind of advertising. On his arrival home he had "Hello U.S.A." written across the sky over New York Harbor. Today almost all the skywriting in the United States is handled by just one company. (See ADVERTISING.)

SLANG "Bring on the *cackleberries*." "He was thrown in the *jug* for stealing a jug of vinegar." Each of these sentences contains slang. In the first "cackleberries," meaning "eggs," is slang. In the next sentence the first "jug" is slang. The second is not.

In a college dictionary about four out of every 100 words are marked "slang." They are words that have not yet been accepted as good English. Perhaps most of them never will be. But some are sure to be. "Bogus," "joke," "mob," and "clumsy" were once slang.

Some slang words are good words used with a different meaning. "Jug" used instead of "jail" is a good example.

Some slang lasts for a very short time. "Twenty-three skiddoo," "vamoose," "beat it," and "scram" followed one another as expressions for "go away." "Goose egg," on the other hand, has been slang for "zero" for many years.

Everything that can be said with slang can be said without it. Then why do people choose to use slang?

Sometimes slang gives us a shorthand way of saying something. "Gas up" is shorter than "fill up with gasoline." Slang is often colorful and forceful. "They are living on a shoestring" makes more of an impression than "They have barely enough money to live on." Some slang words are fun to say. "A couple of bucks" is more fun to say than "two dollars." And some slang is used because the speaker does not want to take time to think of the accepted words for what he wants to say.

All languages have their slang. And in all languages the slang changes.

No one should think of slang as something that should never be used. But there are times when slang is out of place. Slang would be out of place in a sermon or in an address by the president. It would be out of place in a business letter or in an article about atomic energy. And even in ordinary talking it can easily be overdone. Slang loses its effect if there is too much of it.

SLAVERY A man buys a dog to help him hunt. No one thinks anything about it. Everyone has a right to buy a dog. It used to be that people thought just as little about it if one man bought another man and made him work without any pay. A person who belongs to another is a slave.

The ancient Egyptians had many slaves. The pyramids were built with the help of hundreds of thousands of slaves. The ancient Greeks had many slaves, too. At one time the Greeks paid no taxes. Money for government came from silver mines worked by slaves. The Romans also had many slaves. Most of the slaves of early times were people captured in war. A slave might very well come from a richer family and be better educated than his master.

In the early days of the United States many of the people of the South owned slaves. Slave traders brought natives from Africa and sold them. All the slaves of the South were declared free by Abraham Lincoln on January 1, 1863, during the war between the Northern and Southern states.

Nowadays almost no one believes in slavery. No one, we think now, has a right to own any other person. The idea of slavery is an idea the world has outgrown. (See EMANCIPATION PROCLAMATION.)

SLEEP To most boys and girls sleep seems a waste of time. Of course, it is not. We must all sleep several hours every day to keep ourselves strong and well.

When we are working and playing our bodies wear themselves out. In the course of a day, many of the cells our bodies are built of are destroyed. Any rest is a help in letting a person's body get caught up with itself, but sleep is the best kind of rest. When we are asleep our bodies have

All animals do not sleep or rest in the same way.

Mouse

Rabbit

Eyes That Open and Close

Cat

Bird

Fish

Eyes That Stay Open

Insect

Frog

a good chance to build new cells. Even when we are asleep parts of our bodies go on working. Our hearts, for instance, go on beating and our lungs go on taking air in and forcing it out. But both slow down.

Children need more sleep than grown-ups, for their bodies have to grow as well as repair themselves. Babies sleep about twice as much as they stay awake. Grown-ups, on the other hand, are awake about twice as long as they are asleep.

Our brains need sleep as much as our muscles do. Without enough sleep people are likely to be cross and irritable. They forget easily and often do foolish things.

No rule can be made that will tell everyone exactly how much sleep he should have. One person may need more than another even if they are both the same age. Everyone should find out for himself how much sleep he needs to be at his best.

Most other animals sleep, too. Some of them sleep in what seem to us to be peculiar positions. Bats, for instance, hang themselves up by their hind feet. Giraffes sleep standing up. Many birds fasten their toes tightly around branches and settle down over their feet. We close our eyes when we sleep. But not all animals do.

No one is sure exactly what makes people and other animals get sleepy. Perhaps getting sleepy comes from the waste materials that are formed in our bodies when we are working and playing. Perhaps it is mostly habit. Scientists are trying to find out. (See BODY, HUMAN; CELL; HEALTH; HEART.)

SLOTH The sloth is a tree dweller. It lives in the hot, wet forests of South America. This animal spends almost its whole life upside down. It both sleeps and moves about upside down. The sloth spends much of its life holding on to the branch of a tree with its powerful hooked claws.

Once in a while a sloth comes down to the ground to move to a new tree. But it is very awkward on the ground.

The sloth usually hangs upside down in a tree.

Sloths eat leaves and twigs. They move slowly about, usually at night, to get them. During the day sloths spend most of their time sleeping. They doze with their heads between their forelegs and their feet close together. They are so still that they look as if they were frozen into position.

One would think that a sloth would be in great danger from meat-eating animals. But it has one very good means of protection. Tiny green plants called algae grow in its long coarse hair. They make the sloth look from a distance like a part of the tree in which it is living. Its enemies usually pass by without seeing it.

There are two-toed sloths and three-toed sloths. Both have five toes on their hind feet. But a two-toed sloth has two toes, or "fingers," on each front foot, and a three-toed sloth has three. Another name for the three-toed sloth is often found in crossword puzzles. It is "ai" (AH ee).

The sloths belong in the group of mammals to which the armadillo and the great anteater belong. The animals in this group have either no teeth at all or only a few peglike teeth with no enamel covering.

The head of a sloth looks strange, for this animal has no ears that show. It does have inner ears and can hear fairly well. Sloths have no tails.

The word "slothful" has come to mean lazy. It is not hard to see why. (See ALGAE; ANTEATERS; ARMADILLO.)

SMALLPOX A person sick with the disease called smallpox has a high fever and has tiny sores on his skin. The sores are called "pocks." Their small size gives the disease its name.

About 200 years ago a famous doctor predicted that one out of every ten people alive at the time would die of smallpox. He said that one out of every four people would have pitted skin. Smallpox often leaves scars called pits or pockmarks. Now few people have smallpox. The change was brought about by Edward Jenner's discovery that vaccination prevents smallpox.

A person who has had smallpox or who has had a successful vaccination recently enough will not catch the disease. Most people in the United States and in many other countries, too, are now vaccinated. In many places children are not allowed to go to school until they have been vaccinated. Visitors must be vaccinated in order to enter the United States.

Smallpox is caused by a virus. Viruses are the smallest of all disease germs. A person with the disease sends germs into the air by coughing or sneezing or simply by talking. The germs are likely to reach anyone who is nearby. It is important that people with smallpox be kept away from all those who might catch it. Doctors believe that vaccination, together with keeping smallpox patients from mingling with others, may make this disease disappear entirely. (See JENNER, EDWARD.)

SMITH, JOHN (1580-1631) A statue of Captain John Smith stands close to the bank of the James River in Virginia. It is on the site of Jamestown, one of the first white settlements in what is now the United States. Nearby stands an old church tower, almost all that is left of Jamestown.

Jamestown was founded by a group of English settlers in 1607. These settlers were sent out by the London Company. The London Company expected that the settlers would discover gold and silver. But there was no such treasure. Not many of the settlers were prepared for the hard work of clearing land and farming it. Some of the men were quarrelsome. They were not willing to do their share of work.

The settlers had not been wise in choosing a place for their settlement. Boats could anchor easily in the broad James River, but the land around Jamestown was low and marshy. Food was not easy to find or raise. Many settlers were sick. And there was danger from nearby Indians. If John Smith had not taken charge, Jamestown might have been a complete failure.

Smith made a rule that no one could eat who did not work. And he saw to it that the rule was carried out. He had learned to speak Algonquian and could bargain with the Indians for food. Thanks largely to him, the colony lasted.

The best-known story of John Smith is the story of how the Indian princess Pocahontas saved his life. On an exploring expedition Smith was captured by Indians. They took him to their chief, Powhatan. Smith was about to be killed when Pocahontas, Powhatan's daughter, threw herself upon him and begged for his life. Powhatan allowed him to return to Jamestown.

This happening was by no means the first thrilling adventure John Smith had had. According to his own story, his whole life up to that time had been an adventure. He ran away from his home in England when he was only a boy. He was robbed and almost killed while journeying through France. On a boat sailing to the Holy Land he was blamed for a storm and was thrown overboard. He was rescued, however, and soon was in the midst of a war with the Turks. The Turks captured him and sold him as a slave. Again he escaped. He returned to England and from there sailed to America. On the way some of the men on the boat decided to hang him because, they said, he had conspired against the group. Many people think that Smith imagined some of these adventures.

CAPTAIN JOHN SMITH

grims decide where to land. The maps also helped the settlers of the Massachusetts Bay Colony find a place for a settlement. Smith wanted to come back to America with the Pilgrims, but they did not invite him. Neither did the Massachusetts Bay settlers. They told him his "books and maps were much better cheape to teach them" than he himself would be.

As a sort of consolation prize, Smith was given the title of "Admirall of New England." He died in 1631 still hoping to come back to a settlement in the New World.

After only two years in Jamestown, John Smith returned to England. Shortly before he left the colony he was wounded by an explosion of gunpowder. Although his accident did not put an end to his adventures, he was never again in Virginia.

Smith did, however, return to America. Some London merchants sent him to find gold and silver if possible and, if there was no gold or silver, fish and furs. He found only fish and furs, but while his men were hunting and fishing he mapped the shores of what is now New England. In fact John Smith gave the region that name. He did some mapping of the land near the coast, and gave Massachusetts its name.

Smith's maps helped Henry Hudson with his explorations. They helped the Pil-

SMOKE Almost everyone has seen smoke. It rises from chimneys of factories and houses, from bonfires and forest fires, from flickering candles and from lighted cigarettes. Smoke is made chiefly of gases that are produced when some substance burns. When anything burns, it simply changes to some other material or materials. In many cases the new materials produced are gases. Smoke is made largely of water vapor and of carbon dioxide.

If smoke were made entirely of these two substances, no one would complain about it. For both carbon dioxide and water vapor are invisible. True, water vapor when cooled forms tiny drops of water. But no one minds these tiny drops of water. They may make the smoke look white. But often smoke has in it, too, some solid particles

SOURCES OF SMOKE

Factories

Candles

Burning Leaves

Cigarettes

Fireplace

Smoke screens are laid during amphibious landings to help hide troop movements.

of carbon. They are unburned bits of the material that is burning. If there are enough of them, they make smoke dark gray or almost black. If there are fewer, the smoke is less dark.

These tiny particles of carbon may lodge on the walls of chimneys. They are called soot. Too often they escape into the air and settle on the walls and furniture in our houses. Smoke costs the people of the United States millions of dollars every year. More fuel has to be bought to pay for what is wasted in smoke, and smoke adds to bills for laundry and cleaning. Smoke makes a special problem in some cities by helping to form smog. Smog is fog made

darker and more disagreeable by smoke. Many big cities are now working hard to do away with some of their smoke. Smoke and smog may keep a city from being pleasant to live in.

Once in a while smoke is a help. Owners of orange orchards sometimes build smoky fires to keep their orchards from being damaged by frost. In wartime smoke may be a big help in hiding troops from an enemy. (See CARBON.)

SMOKE SCREENS In naval warfare during World War I and the early days of World War II, destroyers often darted in and out laying smoke screens around fleets of ships going into battle. Now smoke screens are seldom used to hide warships. Radar can "see" through smoke and make it possible for gunners to hit hidden targets.

Navies still use smoke screens, however, to protect planes returning to aircraft carriers and to cover beaches where troops are landing. But smoke is even more often used by armies. Troops advancing into battle are sometimes hidden by smoke. So are targets like bridges and airports.

Most smoke screens are made by smoke generators that send forth dense clouds of tiny particles of oil and water. It is easiest, of course, to lay a good smoke screen on a calm day.

Smudge pots are used to protect citrus fruits from frost.

SNAILS There are snails in almost every part of the world. They live in many different sorts of places. There are land snails, fresh-water snails, and sea snails. Snails can be found from high in treetops to deep in the sea.

Snails belong to the big group of animals called mollusks. Like all other mollusks they have soft bodies. Like most other mollusks they have shells. Their shells are all in one piece. In this way they are different from the shells of such mollusks as oysters and clams.

Most snail shells are coiled. They may be long and slender or short and broad. In size they go all the way from shells no bigger than a pinhead to shells more than a foot long. The biggest belong to some of the sea snails called conchs.

A snail carries its shell on its back. When the snail is in danger, it keeps its body inside its shell. As it moves about, its head and its foot are out of the shell. A snail has only one foot. It is big and broad. Most snails glide along slowly on their one foot. But some move in jumps. The queen conch, for instance, has a claw that enables it to go jumping about.

Some snails eat plants. Some eat other animals. Every snail has a peculiar tongue covered with teeth. The sea snail called the periwinkle grows to be only about an inch long, but its tongue is several inches long and has more than 4,000 teeth on it! One kind of snail is a great enemy of oysters because the teeth on its tongue are

Snails make tracks in the sand.

so sharp that it can drill through an oyster shell and eat the oyster.

Snails are a big help in an aquarium. They are good scavengers. And they help keep the walls of the aquarium clean by scraping off the tiny green plants called algae that grow there.

Some kinds of snails are good to eat. Many kinds make good food for whales and fishes. One kind of snail eaten by whales is called the sea butterfly. It rides the ocean waves in great numbers.

Many kinds of snails lay eggs. Other snails carry their eggs inside their bodies until they hatch. Some baby snails look very much like their parents. But others are not easy to recognize as snails.

Garden slugs are close relatives of land snails. But they have no shell except, in some cases, a small thin plate buried in their bodies. In wet seasons slugs may do a great deal of harm to vegetable gardens. They may be a pest in greenhouses, too. (See MOLLUSKS.)

Snails help keep the inside of an aquarium clean.

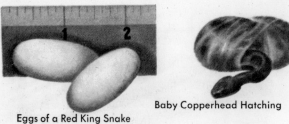

Eggs of a Red King Snake

Baby Copperhead Hatching

SNAKES Almost everybody knows a snake when he sees one. Their shape and their way of moving make them easy to tell from other animals.

Snakes are reptiles. Unlike most other reptiles, snakes are legless. Instead of walking with legs, they walk with their ribs.

A snake's backbone has many more small bones in it than a person's backbone has. Its backbone can therefore bend very easily; the snake can wiggle from side to side or even throw its body into rather big loops. All snakes are covered with scales. The scales on the underside of the body are a big help in moving. The edges catch on the rough ground and keep the snake from slipping backward. Many long, thin muscles move the snake's ribs and backbone. These muscles make it possible for a snake to crawl almost as fast as a boy can run. Snakes can climb well, too. And, oddly enough, they can all swim.

A snake's eyes are always open. It cannot close its eyes because it has no eyelids.

Snakes eat other animals and their eggs. A snake can swallow another animal bigger around than the snake itself. It can do so because its jaws are fastened together with bands that stretch like rubber.

Snakes do not bite with their forked tongues as many people think. They feel

DEVELOPMENT OF RATTLESNAKES' RATTLES

Button Young Adult Old Adult Cross Section of a Rattle

and smell with their tongues. They bite with teeth, as most animals that bite do.

Some snakes are poisonous. They have given all snakes a bad reputation. The only poisonous snakes of the United States are the rattlesnakes, coral snakes, water moccasins, and copperheads. Probably the best known of all poisonous snakes is the king cobra of Asia. The fer-de-lance of South America is another of the well-known deadly snakes. Poisonous snakes have both ordinary teeth and poison fangs. The teeth are not poisonous.

Most snakes are helpful because they eat rats, mice, and insects. The king snake and some others eat poisonous snakes.

As a rule baby snakes are hatched from eggs. But some are born, not hatched.

Head of an Eastern Racer

A Copperhead Shedding

Garter snakes, for instance, do not lay eggs. The mother snake carries her eggs in her body until they have developed into little snakes. When born, the baby snakes are able to crawl about at once.

Snakes shed their skins from time to time. A snake often turns its old skin inside out as it crawls out of it.

A full-grown snake may be only a few inches long. But it may be more than 30 feet long. An anaconda 37 feet long has been measured, and some pythons grow to 33 feet. Big anacondas are also heavy. One may weigh more than 250 pounds.

Snakes are most common in the warm regions of the world. Those that live where winters are cold must hunt for a sheltered place and hibernate when cold weather comes. (See HIBERNATION; REPTILES.)

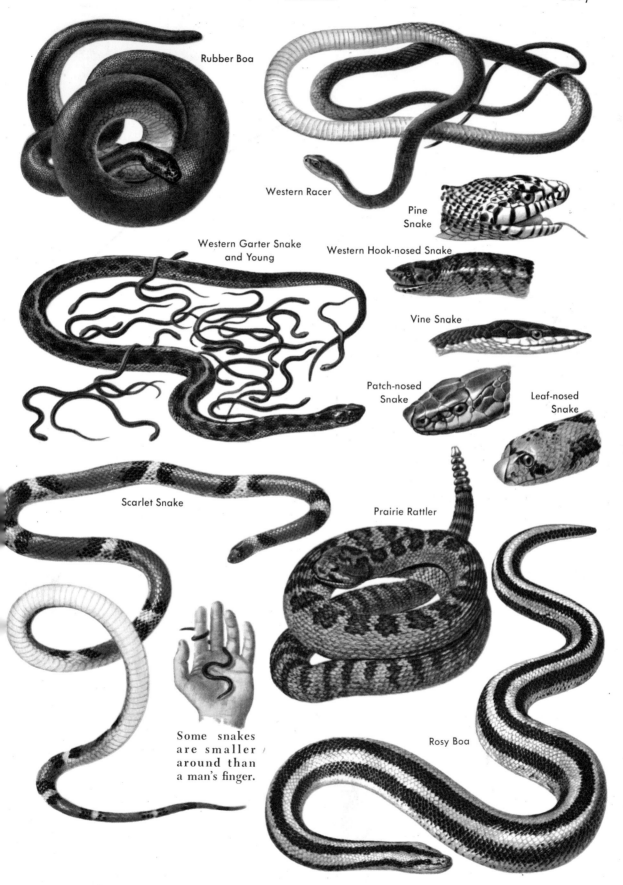

Rubber Boa

Western Racer

Pine Snake

Western Garter Snake and Young

Western Hook-nosed Snake

Vine Snake

Patch-nosed Snake

Leaf-nosed Snake

Scarlet Snake

Prairie Rattler

Some snakes are smaller around than a man's finger.

Rosy Boa

The pattern of each falling snow crystal is different.

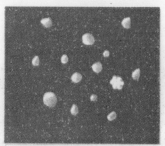

Snow Pellets
(Magnified Three Times)

Ice Needles
Causing Halo

Ice Needles
(Magnified Ten Times)

SNOW Snowflakes are made of tiny crystals of ice. A snowflake may be just one crystal. It may be many clinging together. The big snowflakes that look like little puffs of cotton as they fall are always made up of many crystals.

Snow crystals are beautiful. Most of them have six points or six sides. No two snow crystals have ever been found that were exactly alike. To see their lacy patterns clearly, one has to look at them through a magnifying glass.

Some people have made a hobby of taking pictures of snow crystals. Of course, the snow crystals must be kept cold while the pictures are being taken. If a snow crystal gets warm, it melts, and there is nothing left but a tiny drop of water.

Snow comes from clouds, just as rain does. Some snowflakes fall from clouds more than a mile above the ground. Often the snow crystals are broken as they fall through the air, bumping into one another in their long, downward journey.

It never snows unless it is cold. The water vapor in the air must freeze to form snow crystals. Some people think that it can be too cold to snow. This idea is wrong. It is never too cold to snow.

Snow is sometimes much better for making snowmen and snowballs than at other times. It packs together best if the temperature is about freezing. The snow then melts just a little when it is pressed, and it sticks together well. In very cold weather the ice crystals are frozen so hard that they do not melt as they are pressed together. This snow does not pack well.

A pan that is full of snow is not full of water when the snow melts. It would take about ten panfuls of snow to melt into one panful of water. A great deal of air is caught between snowflakes as they settle to the ground. A layer of snow really makes a kind of fluffy blanket over the ground. Snow is cold, but a blanket of snow often keeps plants and animals from freezing when the air is even colder.

Children are almost always glad to see it snowing. Snow means much fun with sleds and skis and snowshoes. Farmers who have fields of winter wheat are glad to see a blanket of snow on their fields. But snow can make much trouble, too. It slows up cars and trains and planes. It makes it hard for wild animals and animals out on the range to find food. Sometimes food has to be flown to animals that are starving because of a heavy snowfall. Clearing city streets after a heavy snow is expensive. And no one enjoys the snowstorms we call blizzards. (See BLIZZARD; CLOUDS; CRYSTALS; WEATHER.)

SOAP The first bathrooms anyone knows about were built in Crete about 3,500 years ago. In the king's palace both the king and queen had bathrooms of their own. But not even kings and queens in those days could take baths like those we take now. For they had no soap. Soap was not invented until 1,500 years later.

The earliest writer to mention soap was Pliny, a Roman who lived in the first century after Christ. He tells that the Gauls invented soap. The Gauls lived in what is now France. They used soap, Pliny says, to give a brighter color to their hair.

Soon after the Romans heard of soap they began making it for themselves. The little Roman city of Pompeii was buried by the ashes of a volcano in A.D. 79. Nearly 17 centuries later it was uncovered. In it a soap factory was found.

The Romans discovered that soap was good for keeping their clothes as well as their bodies clean. They made their soap from goat tallow and beechwood ashes. Tallow is really fat. Wood ashes contain a chemical called an alkali. Soap is still made by putting some kind of fat and some kind of alkali together.

During the Middle Ages soap was only for the rich. Poor people could not afford it. But no one knew then that keeping clean is important in keeping well.

In early colonial days in America, families made their own soap. They saved all the fat they had left over from cooking. They also saved ashes from their wood fires. About once a month they had a soap-making day. First they poured water through the wood ashes. The water dissolved the alkali in the ashes. They then mixed this water with the fat and boiled the mixture. They boiled it until it was thick. The thick mixture was "soft" soap. If they wanted "hard" soap, they added salt and boiled the mixture longer.

Today, for many purposes, people use "soapless soaps," often called detergents, instead of true soap. But great quantities of true soap are still made, too.

Most soap is now made in big soap factories. These factories make many kinds. Some soap has perfume in it. Some has sand. Some has medicine. Better fats are used for bath soaps than for laundry soaps. One of the better fats is olive oil.

Modern Soap Flakes

Bar Soap

Wooden Spoon

Soapmaking

Old-fashioned Iron Kettle

Soccer Players

Booting the Ball with Head

Defending the Goal

Moving the Ball by Foot

Kickoff

SOCCER

SOCCER The name "soccer" is short for "association football." A hundred years ago the game was called simply football. It was very popular in England. But at that time a newer kind of football was also being played in England. It had been developed at Rugby, a famous English school, in 1823. In the older game the only way of getting the ball down the field to score was to kick it. The newer game allowed players to run with the ball. There came to be much confusion. Often two teams would meet, only to find that one of the teams played by the kicking rules and the other by the running rules.

To do away with the confusion, the "kickers" in 1863 formed a group called the London Football Association. Football played by the kicking rules was, from then on, "association football," or "soccer" for short. Football played by the running rules was given the name of Rugby. American football came from Rugby.

Rules now allow a soccer player to hit the ball with any part of the body except the lower arm and the hands. The goalkeeper may even use these. In a game one sees players hitting the ball with the head, knee, chest, hip, and shoulder. Kicking with the foot, however, is still the most important way of getting the ball down the field. Goals are scored when the ball is kicked between posts at the ends of the field. Goals count one point each.

Soccer is one of the few games that nearly all countries play. Rules, moreover, are almost exactly the same everywhere. The popularity of American football has held soccer back in the United States, but many schools, especially on the east and west coasts, now play soccer.

American football and soccer are not at all the same game, but both are rough. A soccer player is not allowed to tackle or throw another to the ground as in American football. But he may block with his body, and blocking is the roughest part of both games. (See FOOTBALL.)

SOCIALISM The Industrial Revolution of the 18th and 19th centuries was the beginning of a great age of manufacturing. One thing that came about as a result of the Industrial Revolution was the growth of giant industries. Some of these industries today operate mines or oil wells, produce electricity, or run railroads. Others of these giant industries make the cars, television sets, and other things that we consider a part of modern life. Some of the manufacturing companies have more than 100 factories, and hire thousands of workers.

There are people who believe that these giant businesses are too big to be owned by one man or even by a group of people. These people believe that railroads, mines, oil wells, electric companies, and big manufacturing companies should belong to all the people of a nation and should be democratically-controlled. People who hold this belief are called socialists. Their belief is called socialism.

Socialists do not believe that there should be no private property whatsoever. They say there is no reason why people should not be allowed to have their own homes, farms, stores, and small factories. Communists, on the other hand, believe that all homes, farms, and businesses should belong to the nation.

Socialists differ from communists in other important ways. Socialists try to bring about changes in government peacefully—through votes on election day. Communists preach armed revolution to gain their ends. Furthermore, in all countries that are ruled by communist governments, the people have little freedom. Socialists believe in freedom and equality for all people.

Most people accept socialism to some extent. In most cities, for instance, the city owns its schools and its water supply system and its sewage disposal plant. The government of the United States operates the post office. No one argues that water supply, sewage disposal, schools, and carrying the mail should be in private hands.

The word "socialist" appears in the official name of the Soviet Union. Socialists in other countries, however, say that the Russian government does not practice socialism because it allows so little freedom to the people of the country. (See COMMUNISM; INDUSTRIAL REVOLUTION.)

SOCRATES (470?-399 B.C.) One of the most famous men of ancient times was Socrates, a Greek teacher and philosopher. His teachings have come down to us in the writings of Plato, a pupil of Socrates.

Socrates taught that the greatest good in the world is knowledge. He believed that if a man knows what is right, he will do what is right. Men who do evil, Socrates believed, simply do not have the knowledge of what is right. Socrates' method of teaching was to ask searching questions about old beliefs. When his pupils began to examine closely, they began to doubt some of the old beliefs. The great teacher would then lead them to discover what is right.

Unjustly condemned to death for "corruption of the young," Socrates refused to take part in a plot for his escape. To do so, he said, would be evil. As his friends watched, Socrates drank a cup of hemlock —a poison—and died peacefully.

Socrates Teaching

CROSS SECTION OF A FARMER'S FIELD

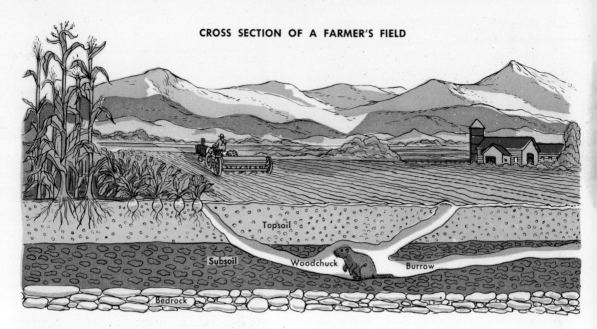

SOIL A handful of good garden soil is a mixture of many things. First of all it has in it tiny bits of rock, probably bits of rock of several different kinds. Then, too, it has the decaying stems and roots and leaves of dead plants. It has the decaying bodies of tiny animals. Probably it has in it, too, many tiny animals that are still alive. Soil is also certain to have in it millions of the very, very tiny plants we call bacteria.

It is hard to grasp how very important soil is. Green plants are the world's food factories. We could not live without them. But plants in turn could not make the food they do without the materials they get from the soil. They have to get water from it, and they must get minerals of many kinds from soil, too.

When the world was very young, there was no soil. The solid rock that made up the land had not yet had time to break up into the tiny bits soil is made of. But now almost everywhere the solid rock has a covering of soil on top. In some places the soil is many feet deep. A covering of soil is usually made up of two layers. The lower layer is called subsoil. It is made up mostly of bits of rock. The upper layer is the topsoil. This is the important

soil, for in it are the tiny plants and animals and the decaying materials mentioned. Some of these are a great help in raising crops.

There are soils of many kinds. This is not surprising, for there are many kinds of rock. Climate has a great deal to do with soil, too. So we have black soil and red soil and yellow soil. We have sandy soil and soil that is mostly clay. We have sour soil and "sweet" soil. Soil can be different in still other ways.

To be good for raising plants, soil must have in it all the minerals plants need. It must have air spaces in it, for the roots of plants need air. Soil must be able to hold water, but it must not hold so much that the roots of the plants growing in it are drowned.

Soil, even very rich soil, wears out if it is not taken care of. The crops grown in it take out some of its minerals. These minerals should be put back. Farmers can put them back by using manure and other kinds of fertilizer. Some of the minerals can be put back by raising clover or some of its relatives on the soil. On their roots these plants have bumps in which there are bacteria of a special kind. These bacteria put nitrogen into the soil.

Much soil is being stolen away from our farms by water and wind. After a heavy rain, water washes soil into streams. The streams carry it to rivers. And the rivers carry it to the seven seas. The great Mississippi River is one of the biggest soil thieves of all. It dumps about 1,000,000 tons of soil into the Gulf of Mexico every day. Of course, at the bottom of the Gulf of Mexico the soil does not do anyone any good. Windstorms from time to time have made dust bowls out of what had been good farmland.

There are ways of stopping our soil thieves. Low-growing plants like grass hold soil in place. Plowing around hills rather than up and down their slopes is a help. Planting such crops as corn in strips between strips of low-growing crops instead of in solid fields helps keep soil from washing away.

What if our soil does blow away or wash away or wear out? Isn't there plenty of rock to make more soil? Yes, there is. But it takes a long, long time to make good soil. The very first farmers used soil that had been millions of years in the making. Scientists tell us that a good thick layer of topsoil is the work of hundreds or even thousands of years. It is very important for us to save the soil we have. (See CONSERVATION; FARMING; MINERALS; ROCKS.)

EROSION

Ocean

Wind Blowing Sand

Careless Lumbering

Stream or River

METHODS OF PREVENTION

Dams for Flood Control

Irrigation in Dry Areas

Contour Farming

Venus in Crescent Phase

Jupiter

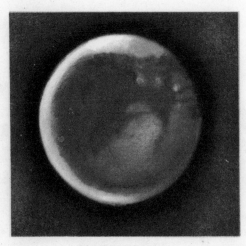

Mars with Polar Caps

SOLAR SYSTEM The word "solar" comes from the Latin word *sol*, which means "sun." The sun and all the traveling bodies around it make up the solar system.

The earth is a planet. In the solar system there are at least eight other planets. There may be more. There may be some out beyond Pluto, the most distant planet that we know about. Six of the planets have moons. The earth has only one, but Jupiter, the giant planet, has twelve. Besides the nine big planets there are at least 1,500 little planets, or asteroids.

In the solar system there are also hundreds of comets, the very strange heavenly bodies that have tails streaming out from them. There are, too, great swarms of meteors. Meteors are pieces of metal or rock, most of them no bigger than grains of sand. Many meteors are pulled to the earth each day. They become white hot when they fall through the air. The small ones are called shooting stars. The largest of them are known as fireballs.

There is only one true star in the solar system—the sun itself. All the other stars are far beyond the outermost planet.

There are a great many heavenly bodies in the solar system, but the space is not crowded. A scale model shows it is not.

Suppose that, out in some great open space, one put a beach ball 30 inches across to stand for the sun. A baseball could stand for Jupiter, a tennis ball for Saturn, and ping-pong balls for Uranus and Neptune. Small marbles would be about the right size for the earth and for Venus. A pea could be used for Mars, and radish seeds for Mercury and Pluto.

Now suppose the scale used in choosing the models is used in placing them. The radish seed for Mercury, the planet nearest the sun, should be 100 feet from the beach ball "sun." The radish seed for Pluto should be 10,000 feet—nearly two miles—from the "sun." The list on the next page shows the distances from the "sun" to the other planet models.

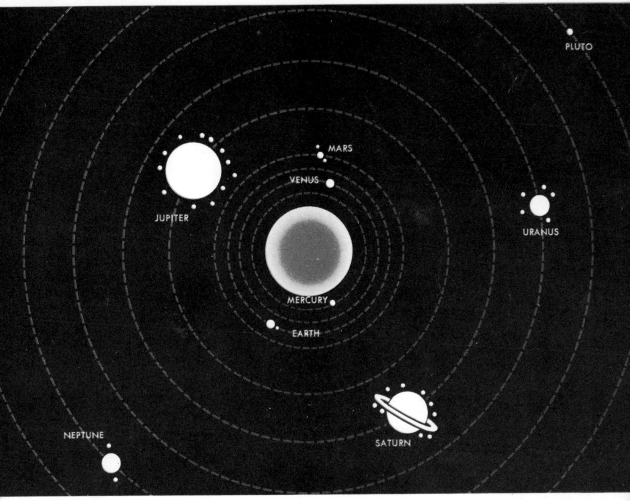

Each planet travels in its own orbit around the sun.

Venus	185 ft.
Earth	260 ft.
Mars	390 ft.
Jupiter	1,300 ft.
Saturn	2,500 ft.
Uranus	5,000 ft.
Neptune	8,000 ft.

The space around the sun would certainly not be crowded! It would not be crowded even if models of all the moons, comets, and planetoids were put in.

The diagram on this page does not give quite the right impression. The space looks much too full. Different scales were used in drawing the planets and in drawing their paths, or orbits. No page in a book is big enough to have the circles for the planets large enough to be seen and to show the orbits on the same scale.

All the heavenly bodies which travel around the sun move very fast. But they cannot run away. The sun pulls them with the mysterious force called gravity.

While all the heavenly bodies in the solar system are traveling around the sun, the sun is traveling through space and taking its family with it. But the sun is so far away from all the other stars that we do not notice any change.

No one knows how the solar system began. One idea is this: In the beginning the sun was surrounded by a great disk-shaped cloud of gas. It whirled round and round as the sun whirled. Gradually material in the cloud formed the planets and the other members of the sun's big family. (See ASTEROIDS; ASTRONOMY; COMET; COPERNICUS; EARTH; GRAVITY; METEORS AND METEORITES; PLANETS; SUN; UNIVERSE.)

Bobolink

box is called a syrinx. It is much like the voice-box we have in our throats.

Birds can be told by their songs. No two birds have songs that are just alike.

Bird lovers have tried to write down bird songs in different ways. One way is to write them in words that give the rhythm of the song. The song of the Maryland yellow-throat is written as "Witchery, witchery" or "Which is it? Which is it?" The song of the whitethroated sparrow is "Old Sam Peabody, Peabody, Peabody." This is the brown thrasher's song: "Hurry up, hurry up, plow it, plow it, harrow it, harrow it, hoe it, hoe it, scatter it, scatter it, seed it, seed it, cover it, cover it, rake it, rake it, push it in, push it in, weed it, weed it, pull it up, leave it alone." This way of writing down a song does not give any idea of the song's beauty.

Another way to write down a bird's song is to write the notes just as the notes are written for the songs we sing. The songs of many birds have been written in this way.

Some birds that have no songs play what we might call instrumental music. The woodpeckers are drummers. Grouse beat the air with their wings. The prairie chicken makes a queer booming noise with air sacs at the sides of its head. (See BIRDS; CANARY; ROBIN.)

SONGBIRDS "Sings like a bird" is a common saying. It is always meant to be a compliment. And certainly anyone that sings like a thrush or a mockingbird sings very well indeed. But not all birds sing well. Some do not sing at all. And some have unpleasant voices. No one would be happy to be told that he sounded like a crow or a loon or a blue jay.

No one agrees as to which songbird is the very best singer. There are many good ones. The pictures show some of the best singers in the United States. The catbird, rose-breasted grosbeak, goldfinch, and meadowlark are other good singers. In the Old World the nightingale is famous for its magnificent singing.

When birds sing they are not singing to us. Instead they are singing to one another. They do most of their singing during their mating and nesting season. Male birds do almost all the singing.

Some kinds of birds seem to have favorite places for singing. A brown thrasher, for instance, perches himself on the top-most branch of a big tree to sing his song.

A bird produces its song in a voice-box which is a part of its windpipe. This voice-

House Wren

These birds are among the best of the songsters, though there are many others which also have beautiful songs.

Cardinal

Brown Thrasher

Song Sparrow

Mockingbird

Hermit Thrush

SOUND PRODUCERS

Firecracker

Phonograph

Men Talking

Trombone

Thunder

Coyote Howling

Drill

Cricket Chirping

SOUND Rustle, rumble, roar; shriek, scream, screech; whisper, warble, whimper; rattle, hiss, slam. These are only a few of the names we have for different sounds. We need many names for sounds because there are a great many different kinds.

Some sounds are soft. Some are loud. Some sounds are high. Some are low. Some sounds are pleasant. Some are unpleasant. But no matter whether sounds are soft or hard, high or low, pleasant or unpleasant, they are all caused in the same way—by the vibrating of something. Vibrating means moving back and forth rapidly.

When leaves rustle, the wind is making them move back and forth. When a lion roars, the vocal cords in the lion's throat are vibrating. Slamming a door makes the wood of the door vibrate.

There are two tuning forks in the pictures. Each one gives out a note when it is struck. But one always gives out the same note. It always gives out the same note because it always moves back and forth the same number of times a second. The other tuning fork is adjustable. It can be made to give out different notes because it can be made to vibrate faster or slower. The faster anything vibrates, the higher the sound it produces. A violinist when he tunes his violin is making the strings just tight enough so that they will vibrate at just the right speed.

Either of these tuning forks can make a very soft sound or a louder one. Hitting a tuning fork hard makes a louder sound than hitting it softly. The prongs move farther the harder they are hit. The farther anything moves when it vibrates, the louder the sound it makes.

Some sounds are so pleasant that we call them music. Some sounds are so unpleasant that we call them noise. The vibrations that make musical sounds are much more regular than the vibrations that cause noise.

Sound is usually carried to our ears through the air. The vibrations of whatever is making the sound set up sound waves in the air. Sound waves in air are a little like ripples in water. But of course we cannot see them.

In air sound travels about 750 miles an hour. When we hear of jet planes traveling faster than sound, we know that they are traveling faster than 750 miles an hour. Seven hundred and fifty miles an hour is roughly 12 miles a minute, or a fifth of a mile a second.

Although 12 miles a minute seems very fast, sound does not travel nearly as fast as light. We therefore see lightning before we hear the thunder it causes.

Although most sounds travel to us by air, they can travel through many other materials. And through some of these materials they can travel better than through air. In a tin can telephone like the one the children are using, the sound travels from one tin can to the other along the string stretched between the cans. Sound travels through iron many times as fast as it travels through air. Suppose a person were standing with his ear against a long iron fence when someone hit the fence about 50 feet away. Then he would hear the sound twice. It would reach one ear through the iron before it reached the other one through the air.

When sound waves in the air hit a solid wall, they may bounce back. There may, in other words, be an echo. Bats guide themselves by producing sound waves too high for us to hear and by listening to the echoes. Sonar systems locate submarines and other objects under water in much the same way. (See ECHO; MUSIC; MUSICAL INSTRUMENTS; PHYSICS.)

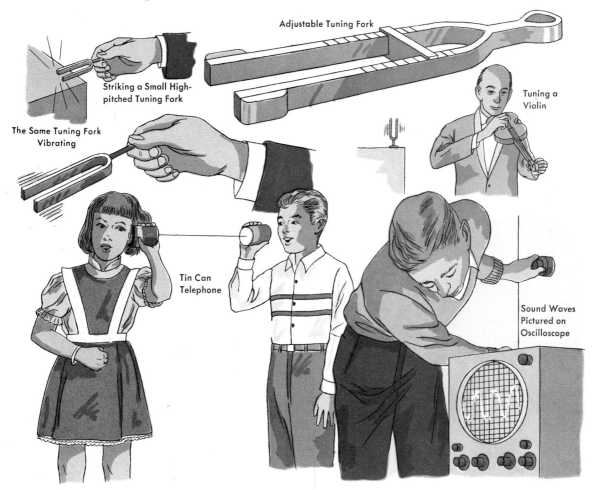

Adjustable Tuning Fork

Striking a Small High-pitched Tuning Fork

The Same Tuning Fork Vibrating

Tuning a Violin

Tin Can Telephone

Sound Waves Pictured on Oscilloscope

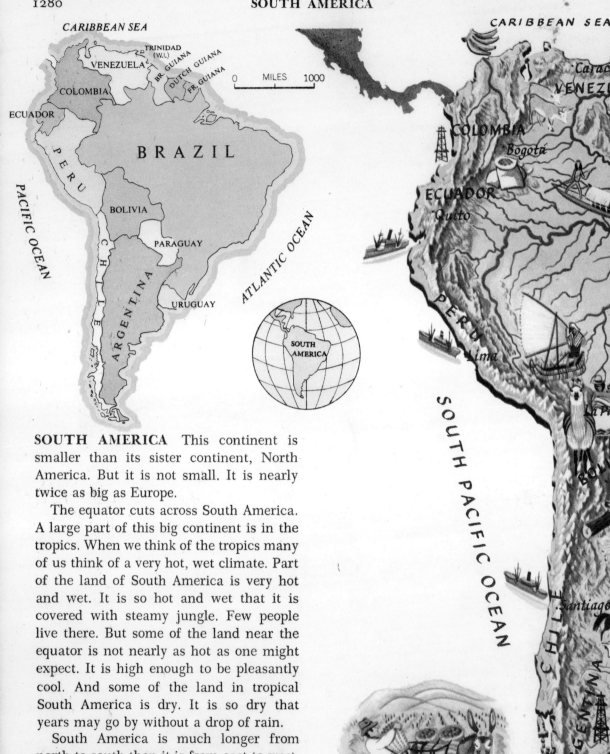

Gathering Grapes in Chile

SOUTH AMERICA This continent is smaller than its sister continent, North America. But it is not small. It is nearly twice as big as Europe.

The equator cuts across South America. A large part of this big continent is in the tropics. When we think of the tropics many of us think of a very hot, wet climate. Part of the land of South America is very hot and wet. It is so hot and wet that it is covered with steamy jungle. Few people live there. But some of the land near the equator is not nearly as hot as one might expect. It is high enough to be pleasantly cool. And some of the land in tropical South America is dry. It is so dry that years may go by without a drop of rain.

South America is much longer from north to south than it is from east to west. It reaches much farther south than Africa does. Its southern tip extends farther to the south than the land of any other continent except Antarctica.

The towering Andes run from north to south down the whole continent. They are

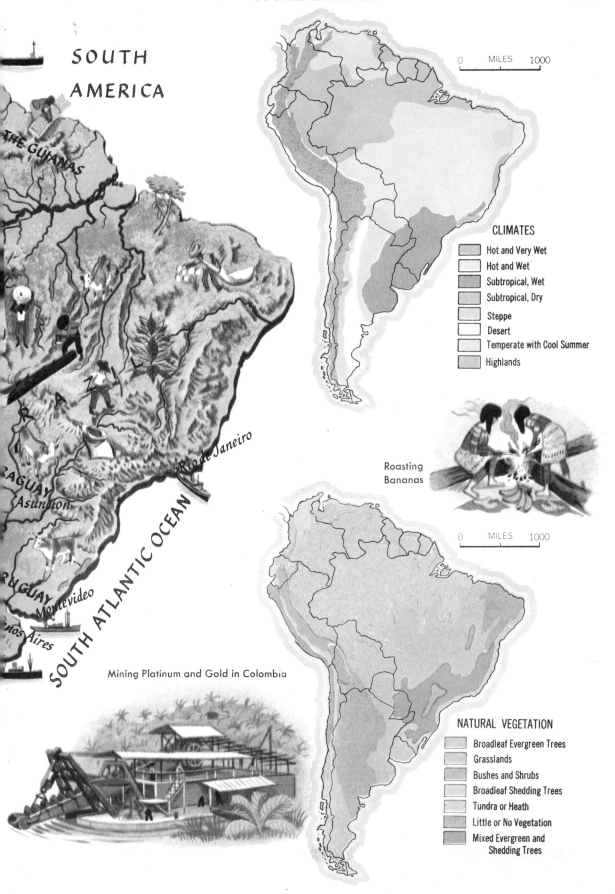

SOUTH
AMERICA

THE GUIANAS

B R A Z I L

PARAGUAY
Asunción

Rio de Janeiro

URUGUAY
Montevideo

Buenos Aires

SOUTH ATLANTIC OCEAN

0   MILES   1000

CLIMATES

- Hot and Very Wet
- Hot and Wet
- Subtropical, Wet
- Subtropical, Dry
- Steppe
- Desert
- Temperate with Cool Summer
- Highlands

Roasting
Bananas

0   MILES   1000

Mining Platinum and Gold in Colombia

NATURAL VEGETATION

- Broadleaf Evergreen Trees
- Grasslands
- Bushes and Shrubs
- Broadleaf Shedding Trees
- Tundra or Heath
- Little or No Vegetation
- Mixed Evergreen and
  Shedding Trees

not far from the western coast anywhere. For a long time they shut the people of the west coast away from the people of the eastern lowlands. Not until the days of airplanes was there any easy way of crossing the Andes.

South America, as the maps show, is divided into many countries. The chart below tells how big each South American country is and how many people it has in it. The size and the population of these countries are given in round numbers.

Much of Venezuela's wealth comes from her oil.

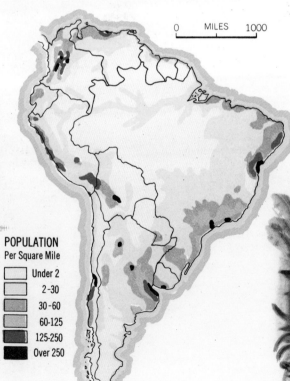

POPULATION
Per Square Mile

- Under 2
- 2-30
- 30-60
- 60-125
- 125-250
- Over 250

COUNTRY	SIZE (in sq. mi.)	POPULATION
Argentina	1,078,000	19,470,000
Bolivia	416,000	3,235,000
Brazil	3,288,000	61,000,000
British Guiana	83,000	499,000
Chile	286,000	6,941,000
Colombia	440,000	12,939,000
Ecuador	116,300	3,777,000
French Guiana	35,000	28,000
Paraguay	157,000	1,601,000
Peru	514,000	9,651,000
Surinam (Dutch Guiana)	55,400	250,000
Uruguay	72,000	2,800,000
Venezuela	352,000	6,000,000

The larger homes show the Spanish influence.

Brazil, the biggest country of South America, is nearly 100 times as big as French Guiana, the smallest. It has more than 2,000 times as many people in it.

All of South America is a part of what is often called Latin America. Latin America is the part of the New World where Spanish or Portuguese, both of which come from Latin, is the common language. Mexico and the countries of Central America are also a part of Latin America.

Spanish and Portuguese became the languages of South America because most of the early settlers in this continent came from Spain or Portugal. Not long after Columbus made his voyages to America, the northern shores of South America were being called the Spanish Main.

There were highly civilized Indians in South America before the time of Columbus. Among them were the Incas of Peru. The Spaniards conquered them and destroyed their civilization. The ruins of their great cities can still be seen.

The story of many of the countries of South America is very much like the story of the United States. They won their freedom from Spain and Portugal just as the United States won its freedom from England. They had patriots just as brave.

A book of many pages would be needed just to list all the plants and animals found in South America. Of course, many of these plants and animals are found only in certain parts of the continent. Orchids and monkeys would be as much out of place at the southern end of South America as a penguin would be in the Amazon. Llamas and alpacas are animals of the highlands. They are in no danger of being killed by boa constrictors, because boa constrictors are found only in tropical forests. The monkey puzzle tree is a South American cousin of the pine tree. It grows in regions of cold winters and warm summers.

South America has not developed as fast as North America. Some parts probably never will have many people. But there is still room in the pleasanter regions for many more people than live there now. South America is a continent with a future. (See AMAZON RIVER; ANDES; BOLÍVAR, SIMÓN; CAPE HORN; INCAS.)

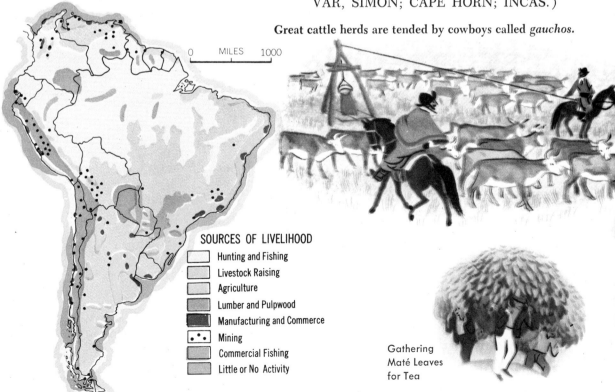

Great cattle herds are tended by cowboys called *gauchos*.

0 MILES 1000

SOURCES OF LIVELIHOOD

- Hunting and Fishing
- Livestock Raising
- Agriculture
- Lumber and Pulpwood
- Manufacturing and Commerce
- Mining
- Commercial Fishing
- Little or No Activity

Gathering Maté Leaves for Tea

SOUTH CAROLINA This South Atlantic state was once part of the huge wilderness Charles I of England named Carolina. The first English settlement in the region was made in 1670. In 1680 the settlement moved to where Charleston now stands, between the Ashley and Cooper rivers.

In time new colonists came. Some were rich planters from the West Indies. Others were French Huguenots, Protestants seeking religious freedom. Later Germans, Scots, and Irish swelled the colony. A few colonists came south from New England.

Much credit is given two men for the early success in this part of Carolina. One was Sir Anthony Ashley Cooper. His system of large plantations worked out well. The other was Henry Woodward, an adventurous young Englishman. A New England ship captain returning from the Far East gave Woodward a small bag of rice. Woodward planted it and in time had a fine crop. He gave seeds to his friends to plant. Rice became the chief money crop on the plantations. Indigo, from which blue and purple dyes were made, was another money crop. In 1729 South Carolina was made into a separate colony.

After the Revolutionary War the planters moved farther from the coast. Cotton then became the important crop. In 1788 South Carolina joined the Union as the eighth state. Plantation life with all its gaiety lasted until the War between the States. Many South Carolinians died fighting for the South and the whole state suffered badly during and after the war.

Today South Carolina is prosperous once more. Some rice lands are now used for vegetables, but a great deal of the warm, rainy coastal lowland is covered with forests again. Much tobacco is now raised. Cotton is still the state's chief money crop, but only half as much land is used for it as before. Fine herds of both dairy and beef cattle are raised.

About 120 miles back from the coast is the Fall Line, which divides the state into

Myrtle Beach

Greenville

State House

Anderson

State Flag

Cypress Gardens

"low country" and "upcountry." The upcountry is an industrial region. But it does not look as if it were. In the valleys are small farms with garden patches and pastures. Many factory workers live on these farms and drive miles to their work each morning. Textile plants employ seven out of ten of all the factory workers. Only North Carolina ranks above South Carolina in textile production.

Many cotton mills were started in South Carolina in the early 1900's, when electric power was developed from the falls along the Fall Line. More electric power, the regrowth of the forests, and modern highways have helped bring more industries. The federal government has a huge atomic energy plant on the Savannah River.

Even with the growth of industry, only one in three people live in cities. The capital, Columbia, is a lively city of nearly 90,000 people. Charleston with its many beautiful colonial houses is one of the show places of the Old South. Here are the Cypress and Magnolia Gardens with gorgeous azaleas and moss-draped live oaks. Charleston's factories show that it also has a part in the state's industrial boom.

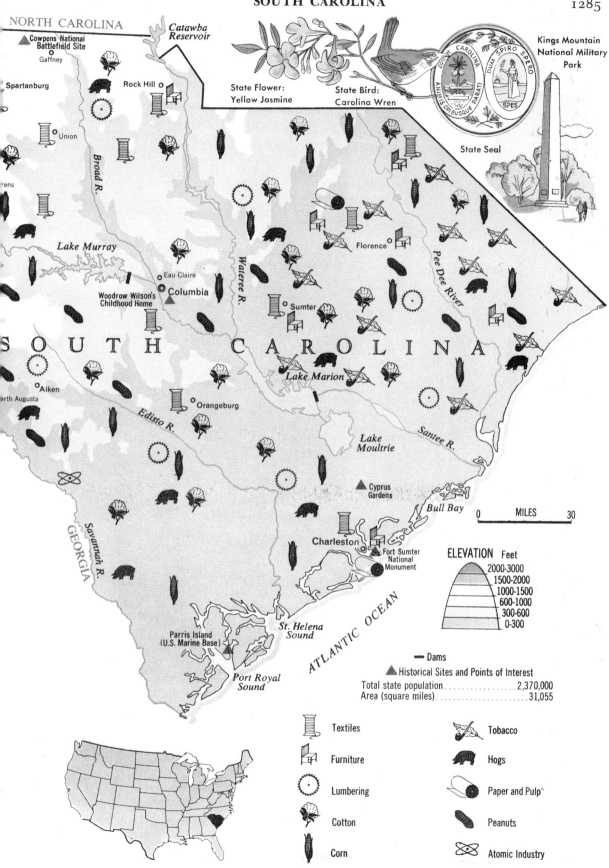

NORTH CAROLINA

Cowpens National Battlefield Site
Gaffney

Spartanburg

Rock Hill

Union

rens

Broad R.

Lake Murray

Eau Claire
Columbia
Woodrow Wilson's Childhood Home

Catawba Reservoir

State Flower: Yellow Jasmine

State Bird: Carolina Wren

Kings Mountain National Military Park

State Seal

Wateree R.

Florence

Pee Dee River

Sumter

SOUTH   CAROLINA

Lake Marion

Aiken
rth Augusta

Edisto R.

Orangeburg

Lake Moultrie

Santee R.

Cyprus Gardens

Bull Bay

MILES   30

GEORGIA

Savannah R.

Charleston

Fort Sumter National Monument

ELEVATION Feet
2000-3000
1500-2000
1000-1500
600-1000
300-600
0-300

Parris Island (U.S. Marine Base)

St. Helena Sound

ATLANTIC OCEAN

Port Royal Sound

━ Dams
▲ Historical Sites and Points of Interest
Total state population 2,370,000
Area (square miles) .31,055

Textiles		Tobacco	
Furniture		Hogs	
Lumbering		Paper and Pulp	
Cotton		Peanuts	
Corn		Atomic Industry	

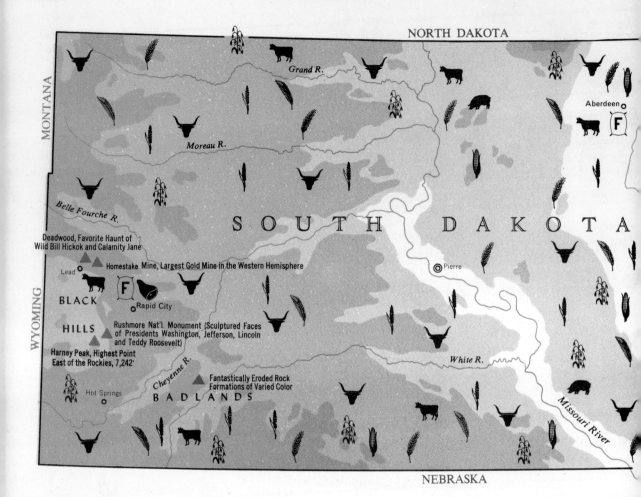

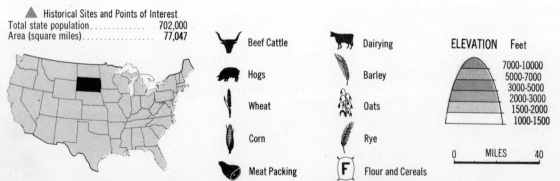

▲ Historical Sites and Points of Interest
Total state population 702,000
Area (square miles) 77,047

🐂 Beef Cattle   🐄 Dairying

🐖 Hogs   🌾 Barley

🌾 Wheat   🌾 Oats

🌽 Corn   🌾 Rye

🥩 Meat Packing   Ⓕ Flour and Cereals

ELEVATION   Feet
7000-10000
5000-7000
3000-5000
2000-3000
1500-2000
1000-1500

0   MILES   40

SOUTH DAKOTA This large state is one of the great farming states of the Middle West. It lies where the prairies rise to the Great Plains. The Missouri River divides the state into two sections: the nearly flat eastern plain, and the higher, hilly land in the west. The state was once a part of the Dakota Territory, named for the Dakota Indians. South Dakota's nickname is "Sunshine State."

Before 1800, fur-traders came into what is now South Dakota. They shipped beaver skins, by way of the Missouri River, to the fur market at St. Louis. In the 1850's, the first farmers settled in the region. Among them were Norwegians, Swedes, Danes, and other Europeans. After 1870, more Americans and Europeans arrived by the new railroads. A gold rush to the Black Hills began in 1875.

State Bird:
Ring-necked
Pheasant

State Seal

State Flag

State Flower:
Pasqueflower

Mt. Rushmore Memorial

Pioneer farmers faced many difficulties in the Dakota country: hot summer winds, dust storms, hailstorms, floods, and grasshoppers. Most of the farmers stayed on in spite of many setbacks.

In 1889, South Dakota was admitted to the Union. Pierre (PEER) is the capital. The state is still rather thinly settled and has no very large cities. Sioux Falls, with a few more than 50,000 people, is the largest city. Two out of three South Dakotans make their living on farms and ranches. The greatest natural wealth of the state is its fertile soil.

East of the Missouri today there are great fields of corn, wheat, and oats, and many cattle and hogs fattening for market. The famous Corn Palace at Mitchell is a sign of how important its corn crop is to South Dakota.

West of the Missouri are vast grazing lands, with cattle and sheep ranches. This region has less fertile soil and receives less rain than the farming region. During most years the livestock can graze in the open, even in winter. But many ranchmen now grow alfalfa and other feed crops by irrigation so that their livestock will have food in severe winters.

The value of South Dakota farm and ranch products is almost ten times the value of its factory and mining products combined. Meat-packing is South Dakota's biggest industry.

The Black Hills in the western part of the state attract many tourists. Highways lead through these hills past beautiful rock formations and high pines. The faces of Washington, Jefferson, Lincoln, and Theodore Roosevelt carved in the stone on Mount Rushmore are very striking. The sculptor was Gutzon Borglum. In the Black Hills is Homestake, the largest gold mine in the Western Hemisphere.

The Bad Lands, in the southwest, also have many visitors. This strange name came from the saying, "bad-for-traveling," which fur-traders used in speaking of this area with its deep gorges and bare, towering rocks. In the Bad Lands, scientists have found the fossilized bones of ancient animals — sabretooths, camels without humps, and horses with three toes.

Like other states of the Middle West, South Dakota is showing signs of change. Farms are getting larger. More work is being done by farm machinery. And factories are growing in number.

SOUTH POLE The South Pole is the farthest-south place on the earth. No matter where on the earth he was when he started, a person who traveled straight south would come to the South Pole if he traveled far enough. The South Pole is straight south of every other place on earth. At the South Pole a person could take a step in only one direction—north.

The South Pole is exactly opposite the North Pole. Like the North Pole, it has night for almost six months of every year and day for the rest of the time. But it has day while the North Pole is having night, and the other way round.

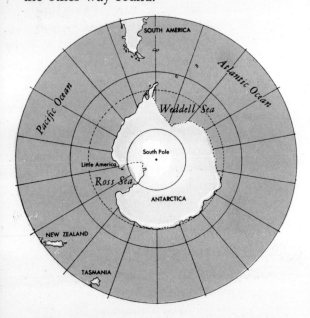

The South Pole is always covered with ice and snow just as the North Pole is. But it is colder than the North Pole.

No submarine will ever cross the South Pole as the "Nautilus" in 1958 crossed the North Pole. The South Pole is near the center of the big continent of Antarctica.

The first person to travel all the way to the South Pole was the Norwegian explorer Roald Amundsen. He reached it in 1911. Before this time other explorers had tried to reach it and had failed. In 1929 America's Richard E. Byrd flew over the South Pole. Both Amundsen and Byrd came to Antarctica by ship. From the shore where he landed it took Amundsen nearly two months to reach the Pole. He traveled by dog sled. Byrd needed only about ten hours to reach it by plane.

Of course, there is no pole to mark the South Pole. Amundsen and Byrd had to find out from the sun and stars when they had come to the earth's southernmost point. (See AMUNDSEN, ROALD; ANTARCTICA; BYRD, RICHARD E.)

SPACE TRAVEL For a very long time people have dreamed of traveling away from the earth to visit the moon and even some of our sister planets. Until recently most people thought that space travel would never be anything more than a dream. But now rockets have gone thousands of miles out into space. And satellites have traveled around the earth.

But before space travel is possible much work must be done. Part of this work is to find out whether people will be able to stand a trip into space.

The rocket ship will have to shoot upward very fast to keep the earth from pulling it back again. We know people can stand great speed—the earth is traveling at the speed of about 66,000 miles an hour. But change in speed is different. A rocket ship, from a standing start, would have to get up to a speed of about 25,000 miles an hour to escape from the earth.

Early in its journey the engines of the rocket ship will be shut off. As soon as "free flight" begins, the traveler will be weightless. The cabin of the space ship will have to be sealed very tight and the passengers will breathe a special mixture of oxygen and other gases. And the space ship will be bombarded by cosmic rays.

Explorers have gone far up into the stratosphere in balloons. There they have had a little taste of what space travel will be like. In laboratories, men have lived for a time under conditions made as much as possible like those space travelers will meet. The records of the breathing and

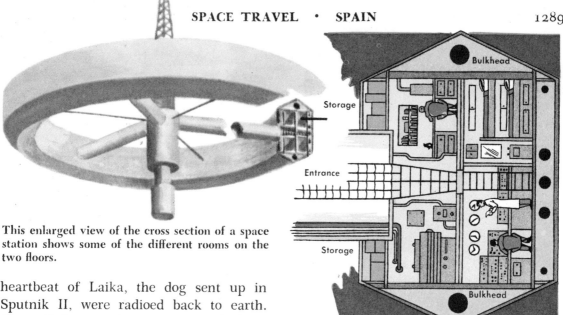

This enlarged view of the cross section of a space station shows some of the different rooms on the two floors.

heartbeat of Laika, the dog sent up in Sputnik II, were radioed back to earth. From all the experiments to try to find out whether people will be able to stand space travel, the answer seems to be "yes."

Unmanned rockets and satellites are gathering more and more information. They have found out about a zone of deadly rays that surrounds the earth hundreds of miles up. This zone scientists now know is shaped like a doughnut. The rockets and satellites have found out, too, that there is not much danger from meteors. Most of them are no bigger than grains of sand.

Space travel would be easier if a space station could be set up several hundred miles above the earth. A number of plans have been made for such a space station. One plan is for a station shaped like a big hollow wheel. This station would have to be located below the zone of deadly rays or else beyond this zone. The first stop for space travelers may have to be the moon.

SPAIN Four centuries ago, Spain was the most powerful country in Europe. Its rise began with a wedding which took place in 1469. The bride was young Princess Isabella of Castile, and the bridegroom was young Prince Ferdinand of Aragon. When they became king and queen, they helped to make a strong Spain by uniting Castile, Aragon, and other lands near by. In 1492 Isabella furnished a poor Italian navigator with ships for a voyage westward on the unknown Atlantic. He was Christopher Columbus. The next hundred years were Spain's "golden century."

The discoveries of Columbus and other explorers helped Spain to secure a vast empire "on which the sun never set." Spanish ships brought home great riches from America. Spain became the mistress of ocean commerce. It came to have not only an empire overseas, but also large possessions in Europe. And Spain's people created beautiful art, architecture, and literature in its golden century.

Later, Spanish kings lost one by one their European possessions. Spanish galleons brought less and less gold. Little Holland became mistress of the seas. In the 19th century, Spain lost almost all of its colonies. Today it is a poor country ruled by a dictator.

The interior of Spain is a large, dry plateau, thinly settled. Farmers in scattered villages of adobe houses grow wheat and raise sheep. In the midst of this plateau stands Madrid, Spain's famous capital and one of the world's great cities. It is a railroad, airline, and trade center. Among its sights are churches and palaces and a great university. Also to be seen there are

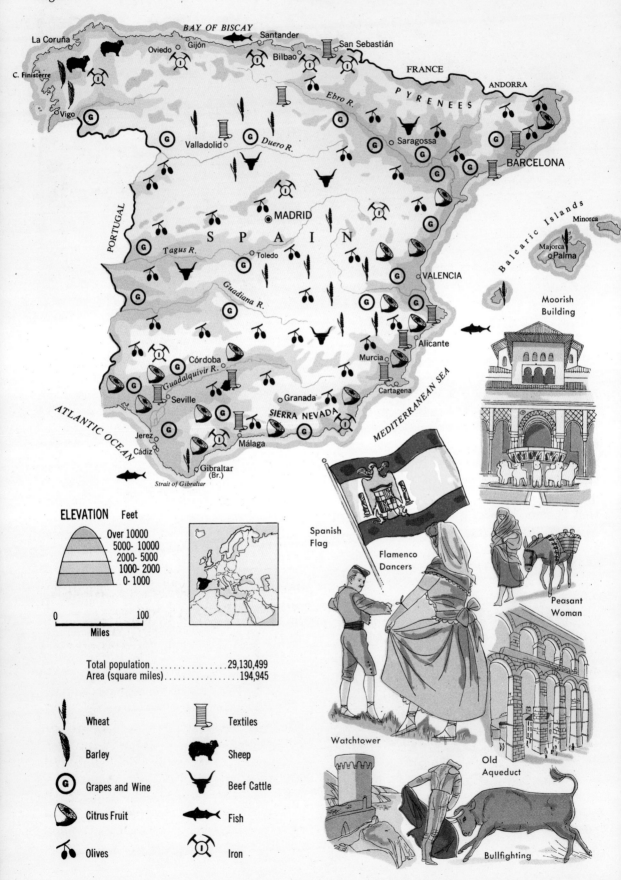

BAY OF BISCAY

La Coruña
C. Finisterre
Vigo

Oviedo   Gijón   Santander
Bilbao   San Sebastián
FRANCE
ANDORRA

P Y R E N E E S

Ebro R.

Valladolid   Duero R.   Saragossa

BARCELONA

S P A I N

MADRID

PORTUGAL   Tagus R.   Toledo

Guadiana R.

VALENCIA

Balearic Islands

Minorca
Majorca   Palma

Moorish
Building

Alicante

Córdoba
Guadalquivir R.   Murcia
Seville   Cartagena

ATLANTIC OCEAN

Granada
SIERRA NEVADA

MEDITERRANEAN SEA

Jerez
Cádiz   Málaga

Gibraltar
(Br.)
Strait of Gibraltar

Spanish
Flag

Flamenco
Dancers

Peasant
Woman

Watchtower

Old
Aqueduct

Bullfighting

ELEVATION   Feet

Over 10000
5000- 10000
2000- 5000
1000- 2000
0- 1000

0   100
Miles

Total population................29,130,499
Area (square miles)................194,945

Wheat   Textiles

Barley   Sheep

(G) Grapes and Wine   Beef Cattle

Citrus Fruit   Fish

Olives   (I) Iron

gay dancing festivals and bullfighting, a famous Spanish sport.

Most of Spain's millions of people live on narrow lowlands near its coast. Near the city of Bilbao, in the rainy northcoast lowland, people mine and export much rich iron ore. And in Bilbao, hydroelectric power, generated in the nearby Pyrenees Mountains, is used in mills in which metal goods are manufactured.

On the east and south along the Mediterranean coasts, and in the valleys of the Ebro and Guadalquivir rivers, much land is irrigated. Famous products of the irrigated farmland are grapes for wine making, and oranges, lemons, and olives.

Spain's chief seaport and factory city is Barcelona. About 1,400,000 people live in it. Only Madrid is larger. Barcelona is famous for its textile mills and its many modern improvements. In many other parts of Spain, lack of enough good roads and railroads has helped to delay progress. Recently, however, many miles of new roads have been built. Some ways of helping farmers get fertilizers and farm machinery have been found. And Spain has many minerals. The future of Spain may well become one of great progress. (See ALHAMBRA; CORK.)

SPEED Our fastest runners can run a mile in a little less than four minutes. But the fastest runner is slow compared with a race horse. A race horse can run a mile in only a little more than a minute and a half. A race horse, in turn, would lose a race to a cheetah, which is the fastest of all land animals. It can cover a mile in less than a minute.

Even a cheetah is slow compared with the fastest birds. A duck hawk, for instance, can fly more than twice as fast as a cheetah can run.

But the fastest living things are slow compared with some of the machines men have built. Automobiles have gone far faster than any animals can travel, and airplanes have gone faster still. For many years airplane builders tried to make an airplane that would travel as fast as sound—about 750 miles an hour. At last they succeeded. The fastest jet planes can travel much faster than sound. We talk about automobiles that go like a bullet, but no automobile really goes as fast. But some airplanes do.

MILES PER HOUR IN AIR	
10	Scissor-tailed Flycatcher
17	Bluebird
36	Robin
45	Homing Pigeon
68	Swift
106	Swallow
120	Golden Eagle
180	Duck Hawk
346	Air Liner
1,405	Jet Airplane
23,450	Moon Rocket

MILES PER HOUR ON LAND	
1	Gopher Snake
9	Chicken
11	Pig
22	Man Sprinting
25	Speed Skater
30	Whitetailed Deer
36	Greyhound
40	Horse
45	Jack Rabbit
60	Gazelle
70	Cheetah
135	Train
210	Motorcycle
394	Automobile
632	Rocket Sled

MILES PER HOUR IN WATER	
1	Pike
2	Man Swimming
7	Salmon
35	Flying Fish (Just Before Takeoff)
41	Ocean Liner
60	Swordfish and Sailfish
248	Jet Speedboat

Rockets are man's fastest devices. The first artificial earth satellite circled the earth at 18,000 miles per hour. And a moon rocket must attain a speed of almost 24,000 miles per hour.

The fastest rockets, however, have yet to come anywhere near the dizzy speed at which the earth goes whirling around the sun. It travels 1,100 miles a *minute!*

Even this speed is a snail's pace compared with the speed of light. The speed of light is almost past imagining. Light travels 186,000 miles a second!

The 20th century is an age of speed. Many modern machines go faster than people of earlier centuries would have believed possible. The next inventions may go even faster.

Spice: the Lure of the East

SPICES The little boxes of spices on our pantry shelves do not seem very important. Of course, the spices make our food taste better. Apple pie is better with a little cinnamon or nutmeg. The dressing for the Thanksgiving turkey is better if it has some sage in it. Pepper helps some foods. But it would not be very hard for most people to do without spices.

The story was different in the Middle Ages. Then spices were so important that dangerous journeys were taken to get them. Great fortunes were risked, too. Wars were even fought to gain control of the routes over which spices were carried. Hard as it is to believe, a man was once put to death because he had sold a stick of cinnamon without permission.

It helps in understanding why spices were so important to the people of the Middle Ages to know that in those days most of our ways of keeping food fit to eat had not been discovered. During the winter the food was very uninteresting. There were no fresh vegetables or fruits.

Meat from animals killed in the fall was usually half spoiled before winter was over. Spices hid any bad taste the food might have. They gave it a pleasant taste instead. No wonder people were willing to pay a great deal for them.

During the Middle Ages spices came chiefly from the East Indies. The East Indies are in the Pacific Ocean close to Asia. The spices were taken from the islands to Asia by boat and then carried across Asia. The journey was a long, hard one.

More than one explorer tried to find an easier way of reaching the "spice islands." In fact, Christopher Columbus was trying to find a shorter, easier way to these islands when he made his famous voyages. But he discovered a new land instead of a new way to the East Indies.

All spices come from plants, but they do not all come from the same part of a plant. Here is a list of some of the most common spices. It tells from what part of a plant each spice comes.

SPICE	PART OF PLANT
Allspice	Berries
Anise	Seeds
Black pepper	Berries
Cardamom	Seeds
Cinnamon	Bark
Cloves	Flower buds
Coriander	Fruit
Ginger	Underground stems
Mace	Seed covering
Mustard	Seeds
Nutmeg	Seeds
Paprika	Fruit
Red pepper	Fruit
Sage	Leaves

Early merchants braved strange seas to get spices.

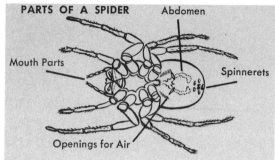

PARTS OF A SPIDER

Abdomen

Mouth Parts

Spinnerets

Openings for Air

SPIDERS Many people have two wrong ideas about spiders. One wrong idea is that spiders are insects. The other is that spiders are all dangerous and that they should be killed on sight.

Spiders *are* like insects in a number of ways that are easy to discover. They are about the same size. They have slender, jointed legs. They are cold-blooded animals with no bones. A tough covering protects them. But there are three easy ways of telling spiders and insects apart. Insects have six legs; spiders have eight. Insects have feelers; spiders do not. An insect's body is divided into three parts, a spider's is divided into only two.

Spiders and insects are different in other ways that are not quite so easy to see. Spiders do not have true jaws. A spider must suck up its food. Spiders have spinnerets with which they spin silk. Some baby insects spin silk from their mouths, but no insects have spinnerets. Spiders have several simple eyes, usually eight. Most insects have two big eyes made up of many simple eyes.

When a spider catches an insect, it sends some poison into the insect with its poison fangs. But most spiders do not produce enough poison to harm a person. Only one spider in the United States is really to be feared. It is the black widow. The black widow is sometimes called the hourglass spider because of the red "hour glass" on the underside of its black body. A person may be made very sick by the bite of a black widow, but usually he gets well.

Spiders are wonderful engineers. The webs they spin are strong. In fact, spider silk is stronger than steel wire of the same size. Some webs are beautiful, too.

All spiders are meat eaters. Insects are the most common spider food. Spiderwebs are very good insect traps.

A baby spider looks like its parents except that it is tiny. Most spiders make a sac for their eggs. When the baby spiders hatch, they must push their way out of the sac. If a little spider gets too hungry before it gets out of the sac, it may turn cannibal and eat up some of its brothers and sisters. As a spider grows, it must shed its skin time after time.

In one way spiders are like camels. They are able to eat enough at one time to last them for many days.

Spiders are air-breathing animals. Some breathe with air tubes much like those insects have. Some breathe with air sacs filled with thin flaps of skin. These air sacs are called book lungs. Some spiders have both air tubes and book lungs.

Spiders are most common in very warm lands. But they have been found in the Far North and on snowcapped mountains.

The picture shows a few of the many kinds. In all there are thousands of kinds of spiders. (See INSECTS.)

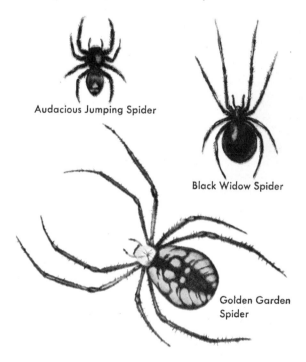

Audacious Jumping Spider

Black Widow Spider

Golden Garden Spider

Weaving Thread into Cloth

SPINNING AND WEAVING Weaving may be older than spinning. Or spinning may have come first. We cannot be sure. The first weaving was probably done with strands of grass or strips of long leaves. It must have been much like the simple weaving children do now with strips of paper. Spinning probably began with the twisting of fibers into cords for nets and bowstrings. Then came the twisting of fibers into thread, or yarn, that could be woven into cloth.

No one knows who found out that fibers from the stems of the flax plant could be twisted into strong yarn. No one knows who first wove flax threads into linen. But we *do* know that more than 5,000 years ago the ancient Egyptians had linen cloth.

An important official in ancient Egypt was the Director of the King's Flax.

Woolen cloth made out of yarn from the wool of sheep was also made in very early times. And one by one other fibers were found that could be spun into yarn and woven into cloth. Some, like wool, came from animals. Others, like linen and cotton, came from plants.

Of course, all early spinning was done by hand. The spinner pulled fibers out of a big mass of fibers. He twisted them into thread, or yarn, by whirling a stick called a spindle. The finished yarn was wound up on the spindle. Spinning wheels like the one in the picture were not made till some time during the Middle Ages. With a spinning wheel the spinner could whirl the spindle very easily.

The first looms for weaving were simple frames of wood. The threads which we now call warp threads were stretched in place on them. Other threads, the weft threads, were laced across them. The ends of the weft threads were fastened to pieces of wood or bone. These "shuttles" made it easy to push the weft threads through from side to side between the warp threads.

When spinning and weaving were done by hand, they were done at home or in small shops. About 200 years ago a great change took place. The spinning jenny

Simple Basket Weave

Spinning on a Spinning Wheel

Greek Loom

American Indian Weaving

Apache Basket

Spinning by Hand on a Spindle

with many spindles was invented. Then came the spinning frame and the spinning mule. Then came, too, the use first of water wheels and then of steam engines to turn the spinning machines. Power looms were invented also. Factories were built, for workmen could not afford to buy big machines for themselves.

The change to power machines came about first in England. It threw many spinners and weavers out of work, because the work of many men could be done by one machine. On the other hand, cloth became so much cheaper that much more of it could be sold. As time went on, more and more workers were needed to run the machines. The use of power machines for spinning and weaving spread to other lands. Some cloth is still woven by hand, but most of it is made by machine. In the United States alone more than a million men and women work in the factories where spinning and weaving are done. They turn out billions of yards of cloth a year on their machines.

Today, besides the fibers from plants and animals, there are many man-made fibers weavers can use. Out of them all, on complicated looms, a great many different kinds of cloth are woven. Some is so delicate that, like ancient silk, it deserves to be called "woven wind." (See FIBERS; INDUSTRIAL REVOLUTION; TEXTILES.)

Bolt of Woven Cloth

Section of a Modern Loom

Enlargement Showing the Warp and Weft

TYPES OF SPONGES

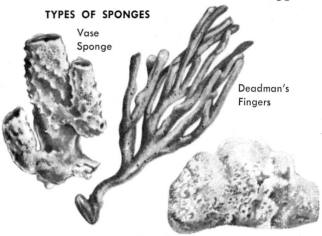

Vase Sponge

Deadman's Fingers

Grass Sponge

SPONGES Funny as it sounds, sponges are the skeletons of sponges. The sponges the skeletons come from are water animals. They are not highly developed. They have no heads or tails; no brains, stomachs, or lungs; no legs, wings, or fins. For almost all their lives they stay in one place. No wonder it was a long time before people discovered that they are animals.

There are hundreds of kinds of sponges. They are of many colors, sizes, and shapes when they are alive. Not all of them have skeletons like the sponges we buy. Some have glassy skeletons. Others have skeletons of chalk.

Even though they are simple, sponges must have food and oxygen. Scattered over their bodies are little holes. Water comes in through these holes, bringing oxygen and tiny plants and animals with it. The water leaves through larger openings.

New sponges may come from eggs. When a sponge egg hatches, the tiny animal swims about for a while. Then it settles down on a shell or a rock to stay for the rest of its life.

But not all sponges come from eggs. A new sponge may simply branch out from an old one. Or a piece that is cut off may grow to be a whole new sponge. Sometimes sponge fishermen cut up sponges and "plant" the pieces at the bottom of the sea.

Some sponges grow in fresh water. But most sponges grow in warm seas.

SQUIDS The largest squids are the largest of all animals without backbones. A giant squid may be as much as 50 feet long. But most squids are much smaller. Some are only six inches long.

Squids are streamlined. They can cut their way through water easily. The small ones are sometimes called "sea arrows."

Around its mouth a squid has ten arms. Two are much longer than the other eight. The two long arms have four rows of suckers. The shorter arms have two rows. The suckers on the arms of a giant squid are as big as teacups. Of course, those on small squids are not nearly so large. With its suckers a squid captures fish and other water animals for food.

A squid has two big eyes. They must be a great help in finding food.

With its fins a squid can swim slowly either forward or backward. But it has a way of moving much faster. It uses jet propulsion. In its body it has a tube called a funnel, or siphon. The opening is underneath the squid's head. The squid can make itself move with great speed by forcing water out of this funnel. If the end of the funnel is pointed forward when water is forced out of it, the squid darts backward. If the end of the funnel is pointed backward, the squid darts forward.

When a squid is trying to escape from an enemy, it usually darts backward and forms a smokescreen around itself with a kind of brown ink. Squids can also change color to match their surroundings.

In spite of their ways of protecting themselves, enormous numbers of squids are eaten by fish and whales. The people of some countries consider squids very good food, too. To cod fishermen squids are important because they make good bait.

Most of us know some of the relatives of the squids much better than we know squids. For squids belong to the great group of animals called mollusks, the group that includes the snails, clams, and oysters. (See MOLLUSKS; OCTOPUS.)

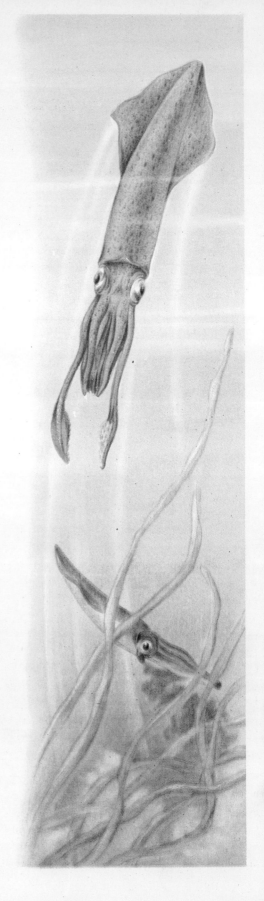

STAINED GLASS It was a day some 800 years ago. In a city in northern France two boys wandered into a small building near a great new cathedral. A man was standing beside a big black iron pot. "May we watch?" the boys asked. The man looked up. "Yes," he answered. "You may watch if you are quiet."

"He is making stained glass for the windows," one boy whispered to the other. "It's a very secret art."

The man poured a mixture into the pot. The boys could see that it was mostly sand. It was not a pretty color. Then the man watched the fire and the pot. He kept the fire burning evenly. Gradually the mixture melted into a thick "taffy."

Suddenly the craftsman lifted out some of the "taffy" on the end of a long iron pipe. He blew through the pipe until he had made the sticky stuff into a big blue bubble. Then, quick as a wink, he laid the blue bubble on his workbench, split it open, and flattened it out. There on his bench was a sheet of beautiful blue glass.

The craftsman explained to the boys that the mixture in the pot was made of quartz sand, a chemical called an alkali, and a compound of a metal. The metal compound gave the glass its beautiful color.

"We do not have many colors," the glassmaker said. "We use a great deal of red and blue glass in the windows and some yellow and green. At times there are impurities in the metal compounds that spoil the glass. And sometimes the impurities give us a more beautiful color than the one we were trying to get."

A scene like this probably took place many times in the 12th and 13th centuries. For that was the time when the great cathedrals were being built throughout Europe and when beautiful stained glass for their windows was being made.

In making a stained glass window the design was drawn on the top of a whitewashed workbench. The colored glass was cut into pieces to fit the design. The cutting was done with a tool called a grozing iron. With this tool, cutting was slow — much slower than the diamond cutting invented later. The pieces of glass were fastened together with strips of lead. The lead made a little frame around each piece. Each piece of glass was about half an inch thick. The light in the cathedrals was beautiful as the sun shone through the glass. People liked stained glass because it was more sparkling and jewel-like than the colored paint in paintings or the colored bits of stone often used in mosaics.

Much of the best stained glass of the great cathedral-building days was made by glassworkers from Venice. The Venetian glassmakers kept some of their ways of getting beautiful colors a secret.

The earliest stained glass windows were just designs in beautiful colors. Then window makers began to make pictures out of the pieces of glass. They began, too, to make clear glass, and paint on the colors they wanted in a special kind of glass enamel. Perhaps the secret of how to make some of the beautiful colors had been lost. Perhaps it was simply easier to get the colors needed by painting them on. At any rate painted glass took the place of the earlier kind of stained glass. Today beautiful stained glass is being made by still newer methods. (See GLASS.)

Al Bloom-Monkmeyer

STAMPS Not long ago a man in New York mailed a letter to a friend in San Francisco. When the letter reached its destination the friend had gone on a vacation trip to Alaska. The letter followed him. It reached Alaska, however, a little too late to catch him. It followed him back to San Francisco, but again it was too late —he had gone to Chicago. It caught up with him there. It had traveled by train and truck and boat. It had been carried, too, in the mailbags of several postmen who make their rounds on foot. The letter

POSTAGE STAMPS

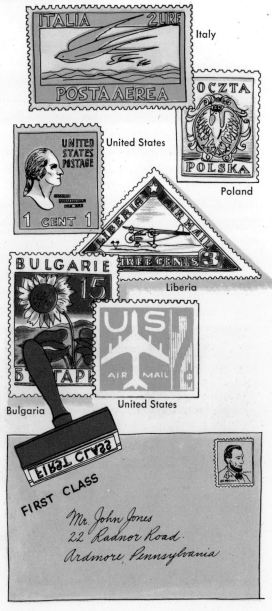

Italy

United States

Poland

Liberia

Bulgaria

United States

FIRST CLASS

Mr. John Jones
22 Radnor Road.
Ardmore, Pennsylvania

was none the worse for its long journey. It had been handled carefully all the way. Most remarkable of all, only a four-cent postage stamp had been needed to pay the letter's way on this long journey.

Postage stamps take billions of letters and packages on journeys every year. All countries issue stamps just as the United States does. Stamps make an easy way of paying a government for handling mail.

The first United States postage stamps were issued in 1847. Since then there have been many, many issues.

Many United States stamps have on them pictures of famous Americans. Among the Americans who have been honored in this way are George Washington, Benjamin Franklin, Pocahontas, Thomas Jefferson, and Will Rogers. In the United States it is against the law to use the portrait of any living person on a stamp.

Some United States stamps call attention to important happenings in the country's history. The founding of Jamestown and the landing of the Pilgrims are two of the happenings that have been shown.

Some stamps call attention to beautiful scenery in the United States. Others call attention to big expositions that are held.

The United States Government prints ordinary postage stamps of many different prices. The cheapest is one-half cent. The most expensive is five dollars. Besides ordinary postage stamps there are air-mail stamps and special delivery stamps.

Many people collect stamps. They pay high prices for stamps that are rare. Some of the most expensive stamps are stamps on which a mistake was made. In 1918, for instance, a few 24-cent air-mail stamps were printed with the airplane upside down. This stamp is now priced at about $6,000! The most valuable of all postage stamps cost only one cent when it was issued. It is a stamp issued in British Guiana in 1856. Only one is left. It probably could not be bought for less than $50,000! (See HOBBIES; U.S. POSTAL SERVICE.)

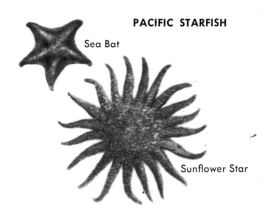

PACIFIC STARFISH

Sea Bat

Sunflower Star

STARFISH The "fish" in this animal's name gives the wrong impression. The starfish is not a fish, even though it lives in the sea. But it is star-shaped. At least, it is shaped much like the stars we draw in pictures. Of course, true stars do not have points; they are huge round balls like the sun.

A starfish when it is first hatched from an egg swims around freely. But soon it settles down to the bottom of the water and spends the rest of its life on the floor of the sea. Sometimes it crawls about, sometimes it rests quietly, and sometimes it burrows down into the sand.

In a starfish's body there are tubes filled with water. These tubes are connected to "tube feet" that end in little suction disks. A starfish moves about on its tube feet. It also breathes through them. Be-

sides, it uses them to help pull open the shells of oysters and clams.

The starfish's mouth is on the underside of its body. As soon as a starfish has pulled open an oyster or clam, it turns its stomach inside out and eats the soft body of the animal it has caught. Starfish eat so many oysters that they sometimes completely ruin oyster beds.

Many people who think they know how a starfish looks have seen only the starfish's skeleton. It shows the starfish's shape. But when a starfish is alive its skeleton is covered with living material. A live starfish may be a bright color.

Some starfishes have more than five arms. But five is the most common number.

Starfishes belong to a group of animals called the "spiny-skinned animals." Scientists call them the echinoderms. Most of these animals have sharp points, or spines, on their outside coverings. The sea urchins, the sand dollars, the sea lilies, the brittle stars, the basket stars, and the sea cucumbers are all in this group. (See INVERTEBRATES; OYSTERS.)

Common or Eastern Star

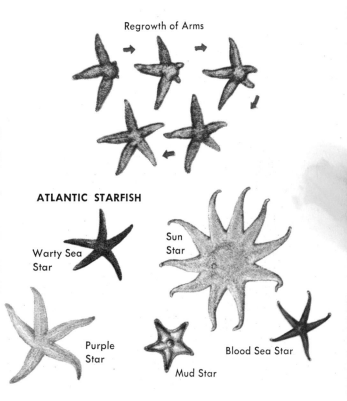

Regrowth of Arms

ATLANTIC STARFISH

Warty Sea Star

Sun Star

Purple Star

Mud Star

Blood Sea Star

Scorpius　("The Scorpion")

STARS The words "sun" and "star" mean the same. All stars are suns. And our sun, along with all other suns, is a star. But when people talk about the stars they usually mean all the stars except our sun. "Stars" is used here as a short way of saying "stars other than the sun."

Some stars are far, far bigger than our sun. Some are smaller. No one can tell how big a star is by how bright it is. Some of the biggest stars are faint because they are so far away.

The sun is about 93,000,000 miles from the earth. Even the closest star is much farther away than that. Light travels 186,000 miles a second. From the sun, light reaches the earth in 8 minutes. It takes light from the nearest star more than four years to reach us! This star is too faint

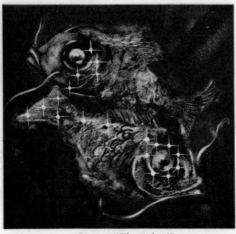

Pisces　("The Fishes")

to be seen without a telescope. The name of this star is Proxima Centauri.

Sirius, the Dog Star, is the brightest star in the sky. It takes nearly nine years for light from this star to reach us. If Sirius should explode tonight, it would be nearly nine years before we saw the explosion.

Even Sirius is a near neighbor compared with some of the other bright stars. It takes light from the brilliant star Rigel more than 500 years to reach us. The light that reaches the earth tonight from Rigel left that star before Columbus discovered America. It is hard to imagine how far away some of the faint stars are.

When we say that anything is star-shaped we mean that it has five points. But

Ursa Major　("The Great Bear")

stars are really big round balls like our sun. People got the idea that stars have points because they twinkle. It is the air that makes them do so. If we could see them from the moon, where there is no air, they would shine with a steady light.

Like the sun, stars are all great shining balls, but they are not all single balls. Thousands of the stars in our sky are double-suns. They are made of two stars that travel around and around each other. Some "stars" are really systems of more than two suns. What we see as a star may even be six suns traveling around one another.

Stars are not all the same color. Some are bluish-white, some white, some yellow, some orange, and some red. They are different colors because some are hotter than others. The bluish-white ones are the hottest. Next come the white, then the yellow, then the orange, and then the red. But even the red stars are so hot that it is hard to imagine how hot they are.

We see stars only at night. But we could see them in the daytime if the sunlit air did not hide them. There are stars in all directions from the earth.

On a clear night a person who looks up at the sky sees about 2,000 separate stars. Not many thousands of stars are bright enough to be seen without a telescope. But telescopes tell us that there are millions and millions and millions of stars. There are probably as many stars as there are grains of sand on all the world's seashores.

The stars we see are not spread evenly over the sky. Instead they are in groups, called constellations. The people of long ago thought that the different constellations made pictures in the sky. The names they gave the constellations tell us what pictures they saw.

Scientists divide stars into groups according to their brightness. The 20 brightest stars are called "first magnitude" stars. These 20 stars are in 18 different constellations. The following list names the first magnitude stars in order of brightness and tells in what constellation each one belongs. (See ASTRONOMY; CONSTELLATIONS; LIGHT; NORTH STAR; SOLAR SYSTEM; SUN; TELESCOPE; ZODIAC.)

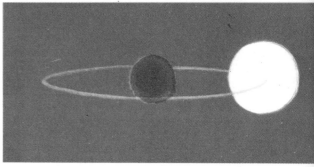

Some stars are double and revolve around each other.

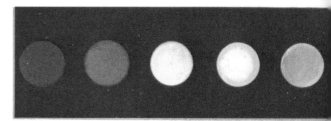

Star colors vary from red (the coolest) to blue-white (the hottest visible stars).

STAR	CONSTELLATION
Sirius	Canis Major ("The Great Dog")
Canopus	Argo ("The Ship")
Alpha Centauri	Centaur ("The Centaur")
Vega	Lyra ("The Lyre")
Capella	Auriga ("The Charioteer")
Arcturus	Boötes ("The Herdsman")
Rigel	Orion ("The Hunter")
Procyon	Canis Minor ("The Little Dog")
Achernar	Eridanus ("The River")
Beta Centauri	Centaur ("The Centaur")
Altair	Aquila ("The Eagle")
Betelgeuse	Orion ("The Hunter")
Alpha Crucis	Crux ("The Cross")
Aldebaran	Taurus ("The Bull")
Pollux	Gemini ("The Twins")
Spica	Virgo ("The Virgin")
Antares	Scorpius ("The Scorpion")
Fomalhaut	Piscis Austrinus ("The Southern Fish")
Deneb	Cygnus ("The Swan")
Regulus	Leo ("The Lion")

A star "twinkles" because its light is bent and scattered by our atmosphere.

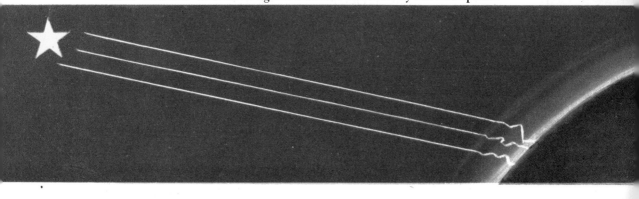

STATESMEN Some of the men who are famous in history are remembered because they explored new lands, worked out new inventions, or won great victories in war. Some men are famous because they wrote great books, painted beautiful pictures, or composed wonderful music. And some men won fame because of what they achieved in the field of government. Such men are called statesmen.

Many systems of government have been tried during man's history. Some statesmen have served governments that most people would consider good. Other men have served governments that would be considered oppressive. But whether men have served good or bad governments, if their actions have changed the course of history, they are remembered. The world is different because they lived.

NAME	NATIONALITY AND DATES	
Machiavelli, Niccolò Italian Political Writer	Italian 1469-1527	Machiavelli won world fame for the ideas of government that he put forth in his book The Prince.
Richelieu, Armand Jean du Plessis, Duc de First Minister of France	French 1585-1642	Richelieu unified the French government into an absolute power which was centered around himself and King Louis XIII.
Cromwell, Oliver Lord Protector of England	English 1599-1658	Cromwell led the Puritan armies in their revolt against the English king. He governed England from 1649 to 1658.
Mazarin, Jules, Cardinal First Minister of France	French 1602-1661	Mazarin succeeded Richelieu as the king's chief minister. He helped Louis XIV keep absolute power over France.
Walpole, Sir Robert Prime Minister of Great Britain	English 1676-1745	Walpole, "the first English prime minister," persuaded George I and George II to give up some of their power to him.
Franklin, Benjamin American Patriot	American 1706-1790	Franklin worked for American independence. He also helped strengthen the government of the early United States.
Pitt, William, Earl of Chatham Member of Parliament	English 1708-1778	Pitt urged that the people in the American colonies be given the same constitutional rights that other Englishmen had.
Burke, Edmund Member of Parliament	English 1729-1797	Burke, in the British Parliament, urged fairer treatment for the American colonies. He wanted to avoid a revolution.
Washington, George U.S. President	American 1732-1799	Washington led the colonies in their revolt against England. He helped unify the United States in its difficult early years.
Jefferson, Thomas U.S. President	American 1743-1826	Jefferson wrote into the Declaration of Independence the principles of democracy on which the United States was founded.
Madison, James U.S. President	American 1751-1836	Madison helped write the United States Constitution. He was president during the War of 1812 against England.
Talleyrand, Charles Maurice de Foreign Minister of France	French 1754-1838	Talleyrand succeeded in regaining for France her position as a leading nation after Napoleon had been defeated.
Monroe, James U.S. President	American 1758-1831	Monroe, while president, issued the Monroe Doctrine, warning European nations not to colonize or interfere in the Americas.
Pitt, William Prime Minister of Great Britain	English 1759-1806	Pitt tried to reform the British government but had to abandon many of his ideas at the outbreak of the Napoleonic Wars.
Metternich, Prince Klemens von Foreign Minister of Austria	Austrian 1773-1859	Metternich, in order to protect Austria, tried to arouse other European nations against Napoleon.
Clay, Henry U.S. Senator	American 1777-1852	Clay's aim was "the preservation of the Union" through peaceful settlement of the slavery question.
Calhoun, John C. U.S. Vice-President	American 1782-1850	Calhoun opposed having a strong federal government. He believed that each state should decide most things for itself.
Webster, Daniel U.S. Senator	American 1782-1852	Webster, through the power of his speeches in the Senate, helped keep the North and South from war for 30 years.
Bolívar, Simón South American Liberator	Venezuelan 1783-1830	Bolívar is called "the Liberator" because he led the armies that freed Colombia, Ecuador, Peru, and Venezuela from Spain.

NAME	NATIONALITY AND DATES	
Disraeli, Benjamin Prime Minister of Great Britain	English 1804-1881	Disraeli worked for the expansion of English territories. An empire was created "on which the sun never sets."
Garibaldi, Giuseppe Italian Patriot	Italian 1807-1882	Garibaldi spent much of his life helping to free the Italian Peninsula from Austrian, French, and Spanish rule.
Gladstone, William E. Prime Minister of Great Britain	English 1809-1898	Gladstone brought about important reforms in the British civil service, voting system, army, education, and courts.
Lincoln, Abraham U.S. President	American 1809-1865	Lincoln freed the slaves during the War between the States. He led the struggle to preserve the Union.
Cavour, Conte Camillo Benso di Premier of Sardinia	Italian 1810-1861	Cavour was the most important figure in uniting the small states of the Italian Peninsula into one nation.
Bismarck, Prince Otto Eduard Leopold von Chancellor of Germany	German 1815-1898	Bismarck formed the German nation by unifying a group of small states. He governed it through the use of force.
Macdonald, Sir John A. Prime Minister of Canada	Canadian 1815-1891	Macdonald was a leader in creating the Dominion of Canada out of the British North American provinces.
Clemenceau, Georges Premier of France	French 1841-1929	Clemenceau was premier during World War I and led the French delegation at the peace conference at Versailles.
Wilson, Woodrow U.S. President	American 1856-1924	Wilson was the leading figure in founding the League of Nations. He could not, however, get the United States to join.
Roosevelt, Theodore U.S. President	American 1858-1919	Roosevelt fought to break up powerful business groups in order to bring about freer business competition.
Lloyd George, David Prime Minister of Great Britain	English 1863-1945	Lloyd George led the British during World War I and was head of the British delegation to the Versailles Conference.
Gandhi, Mahatma (Mohandas Karamchand Gandhi) Indian Patriot	Indian 1869-1948	Gandhi struggled to free India from English rule. He tried to achieve his goal by peaceful rather than violent means.
Lenin, Nikolai (Vladimir Ilich Ulyanov) Communist Leader	Russian 1870-1924	Lenin was the first communist leader of Russia after the Bolshevik Revolution of 1917.
Churchill, Sir Winston Leonard Spencer Prime Minister of Great Britain	English 1874-	Churchill, during World War I, held important government posts. As prime minister, he led England to victory in World War II.
Stalin, Joseph (Iosif Vissarionovich Dzhugashvili) Communist Leader	Russian 1879-1953	Stalin followed Lenin as head of the Russian Communist Party. He greatly extended the power of the U.S.S.R.
Roosevelt, Franklin Delano U.S. President	American 1882-1945	Roosevelt had to deal with the United States' most serious depression. He also led the nation during World War II.

Richelieu
French

Bismarck
German

Gladstone
English

Gandhi
Indian

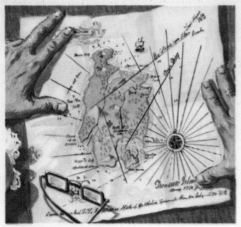

An X marked the treasure on the map.

STEVENSON, ROBERT LOUIS (1850-1894) The famous author Robert Louis Stevenson was born in Edinburgh, Scotland. Even as a child his health was poor, and much of his life was spent in trying to find a place to live where he would feel better. His parents were wealthy. He was an only child. One of the closest friends of his childhood was the nurse who cared for him during the months he spent in bed.

Stevenson studied engineering and law, but both were too strenuous for him. Then he began to write essays for magazines. He traveled a great deal in France, Germany, and Scotland, and made two trips to the United States. In San Francisco he married an American woman whom he had met earlier in France.

A Child's Garden of Verses, which recalls many happy times in his own childhood, is dedicated to his old nurse. The poems were later set to music. Many boys and girls enjoy them today.

Treasure Island was the book that made Stevenson famous. One day he drew a map of an imaginary island. He called it "Treasure Island." After a while he wrote a story about the island for his young stepson. The book became a great favorite of readers young and old.

Stevenson also wrote *Kidnapped,* the story of a boy named David Balfour, who was one of Stevenson's own ancestors. The later adventures of the same boy were told in the book *David Balfour.*

After a cruise in the South Seas, Stevenson settled in the Samoan Islands. The natives called him Tusitala, meaning "teller of tales." When he died, the natives carried Stevenson to the top of Mount Vaea and buried him as one of their chiefs. (See ENGLISH WRITERS.)

Black Arrow

Kidnapped

David Balfour

During a hurricane, the high winds and lashing rains cause a great deal of damage

STORMS "Hurricane Hits Florida," "Tornado Wipes Out Texas Town," "Ice Storm Tears Down Telephone Lines." Often our newspapers have headlines like these. Big storms are always news.

Hurricanes are great wind storms. They are hundreds of miles across. The wind rushes into the center of a hurricane from all sides. It may reach a speed of nearly 200 miles an hour. The center of a hurricane is called its eye. People are often fooled when the eye of a hurricane reaches them. The wind dies down, and they think that the storm is over. Then the wind begins to blow furiously again. A hurricane may last for 24 hours at one place.

Hurricanes are tropical storms. The Canary Islands near Africa are sometimes called the "hatching place" of hurricanes. Most of them start from near there. They move westward across the Atlantic. When they strike land they may do great damage. But now the weatherman always knows when one is on the way. He can send out warnings about it. People can board up their windows and do many other such things to protect themselves if they know about a hurricane in time.

North of the equator there are on the average only five or six hurricanes a year. They are most likely to occur in the months of August and September.

Hurricanes are given girls' names by the United States Weather Bureau. The first hurricane of a season has a name that begins with A, the name of the second begins with B, and so on. "Diane" in 1955 did damage amounting to 700 million dollars and caused the death of 184 people.

Typhoons are like hurricanes. But they are Pacific Ocean storms.

Tornadoes are wind storms, too. A tornado oftens tears down everything in its path. The wind may be blowing more than 300 miles an hour. Tornadoes are sometimes called twisters. The wind whirls round and round as it rushes into the center. A tornado cloud is funnel-shaped. It is often very black because so much dirt has been sucked up into it.

Although violent, tornadoes are small storms. Their paths may not be more than a quarter of a mile wide.

Tornadoes move very fast. A tornado usually does not last more than half a minute at any one spot. The weatherman can-

The eye, or center, of a hurricane is calm.

DEVELOPMENT
OF A
TORNADO

Storm clouds form.

Funnel forms as tornado develops.

Funnel sucks up dust and debris.

A tornado can drive a straw into a tree.

Waterspout forms in a tornado over the ocean.

not warn people of every tornado. They form too quickly and move too fast. But the weatherman can tell people when the conditions are right for tornadoes. Tornadoes come most often in the spring.

Many strange things happen in tornadoes. A house may be lifted up and carried away without hurting the people in it. Furniture may be blown out of one house and into another.

A heavy snow slows down city activities.

There are sometimes tornadoes out at sea. They are called waterspouts.

The wind may blow hard for a few minutes in a thunderstorm. But thunderstorms are not such violent storms as tornadoes and hurricanes. It is good they are not, for thunderstorms are common. In the whole world there are about 40,000 every day.

These storms get their name from the lightning and thunder that come with them. They are small storms. There is often a thunderstorm in one part of a city but not in another part. On land thunderstorms come most often in summer. They are more common in winter over the sea.

Blizzards are snowstorms with strong winds. The chief danger in blizzards is of getting lost and being buried in the snow.

Sandstorms are one of the dangers caravans meet in crossing the deserts. Camels are good desert animals partly because they have ways of keeping sand out of their eyes and ears during a sandstorm.

Dust storms are much like sandstorms. They blow away a great deal of good soil. Many people get sick from breathing dust during these storms.

Ice storms are most likely to come when the temperature is just a little below freezing. Rain freezes as it strikes trees and bushes and telephone wires. Every twig and wire gets a coating of ice. The out-of-doors looks like fairyland. Ice storms may leave broken wires and branches behind them, but they are beautiful while they last. (See BLIZZARD; METEOROLOGY; U.S. WEATHER BUREAU; WIND.)

Thunderstorm clouds reach great heights.

STRAITS A strait is a narrow water passageway that joins two big bodies of water. It is just the opposite of an isthmus. Some canals are man-made straits. The Suez and Panama canals are two of them.

At the same time that a strait joins two bodies of water, it separates two bodies of land. It may separate two countries, two continents, or an island from the mainland.

A few straits are called rivers. Part of the city of New York is built on the island of Manhattan. The East River is on one side of the island. This river is really a strait.

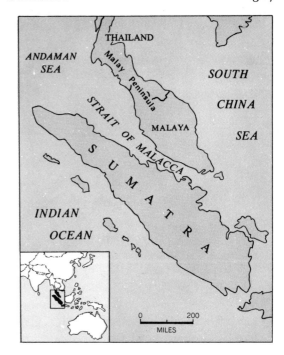

Straits have been very important in the history of the world. Since they are narrow, they can be guarded rather easily. Enemy ships can be attacked as they try to pass through. Many straits have forts near by.

Some straits are parts of great trade routes. The peace of the world depends partly on how these straits are controlled. The chart names 10 of the world's important straits. (See BOSPORUS; DARDANELLES; GIBRALTAR; ISTHMUS.)

STRAIT	JOINING	SEPARATING
Bab el Mandeb	Red Sea— Indian Ocean	Africa— Arabia
Bering	Bering Sea— Arctic Ocean	Alaska— Soviet Union
Bosporus	Black Sea— Sea of Marmara	Europe— Asia Minor
Dardanelles	Aegean Sea— Sea of Marmara	Europe— Asia Minor
Dover	English Channel North Sea	England— France
Formosa	South China Sea— East China Sea	China— Taiwan(Formosa)
Gibraltar	Atlantic Ocean— Mediterranean Sea	Spain— Morocco
Golden Gate	Pacific Ocean— San Francisco Bay	California
Mackinac	Lake Michigan— Lake Huron	Michigan
Magellan	Atlantic Ocean— Pacific Ocean	South America— Tierra del Fuego

The lute was used by medieval singers.

STRINGED INSTRUMENTS The family of stringed instruments used in a symphony orchestra is made up of the violin, viola, violoncello, and double bass. They all look much alike except for size, and they are all played in a similar way. They all have four strings, with the exception of the double bass, which can have three, four, or five strings. Each string is tuned to a different sound, or pitch.

The violin is the smallest member of the family. It has a high, or soprano, voice. The viola is next in size and has a slightly lower, or alto, voice. Both of them are held under the chin when they are being played. The violoncello, or cello, is quite a bit larger and has a tenor and baritone voice. It must be played by setting it on the floor between the knees of the player. The double bass is the grandfather of them all, with a big, bass voice. It is so

The koto is a Japanese stringed instrument.

large that the player must stand up or sit on a tall stool to play it.

Stringed instruments are usually played by drawing a bow over the strings, but the strings can also be plucked. The bow is made of a thin, strong stick with a band of horsehair firmly stretched from end to end. The violin bow is about 28 inches long. Bows for the larger instruments are shorter and heavier. The bows are usually drawn over the strings with the right hand.

The horsehairs on bows are rubbed with rosin so they will "catch" the strings and cause them to move back and forth rapidly. This kind of motion, which is called vibration, produces sound. In the hollow part of the instrument—the sound box—the

The banjo was often heard in the old South.

sound is made louder, or amplified, so that it can be heard easily.

The pitch of each string can be made higher by pressing the string down against the finger board with the fingers of the left hand. Pressing the string down shortens the part that is free to vibrate over the sound box.

The violin is not an ancient instrument like the flute or the harp, but it is older than the piano. The violin as we know it today is about 400 years old. Some of the best instruments of the violin family that we have were made over 200 years ago by the great Italian violin makers Amati, Stradivarius, and Guarnerius.

Harps have changed in size and shape.

Jazz and symphony orchestras use the large double bass.

The cello has a full, golden tone.

The harp is another stringed instrument used in symphony orchestras. It is an ancient instrument and is mentioned often in the Bible. The modern harp has 47 strings that are tuned to produce a regular major scale. The player can vary the note of each string by shortening the strings. He does this by using foot pedals. The instrument is always plucked.

Years ago there were hundreds of different instruments, each with a special sound of its own. Though these old instruments often have a beautiful tone, they do not sound loudly enough to mix well with the other instruments of a large modern orchestra. Some of these ancient instruments—the viols—were developed into the modern violin family.

The mandolin, guitar, banjo, and ukulele have from four to eight strings. They are played by plucking. These instruments are either played alone or used to accompany the human voice.

One other very common instrument, the piano, has strings, but its strings do not show. It is not usually called a stringed instrument because its strings are not plucked or made to vibrate with a bow. Instead, they are made to vibrate by little felt hammers. In this sense, the piano is like a percussion instrument. (See MUSIC; MUSICAL INSTRUMENTS; ORCHESTRA; PERCUSSION INSTRUMENTS; PIANO; WIND INSTRUMENTS.)

Hawaiian Guitar

The viola is slightly larger than the violin and plays five notes lower

The violin was developed from the medieval viol.

SUBMARINES

The atomic-powered "Nautilus" sailed under the North Pole without surfacing.

SUBMARINES In 1870 Jules Verne wrote a story called *Twenty Thousand Leagues Under the Sea.* It told about the long trips of Captain Nemo and his crew in his submarine "Nautilus." At that time no one had built a submarine that could stay under water for weeks at a time or one that would carry many people. In 1954 the U.S. Navy added a real submarine "Nautilus" to its fleet. It was the first submarine driven by atomic power. In August, 1958, the "Nautilus" made history by traveling under the ice across the North Pole.

"Submarine" is a good name for a boat that can travel under water. The word means "under the sea." During the World Wars submarines were called U-boats. This name comes from *unterseeboot,* the German word for "undersea boat."

Fish are nature's submarines. They are streamlined so that they can cut their way through water easily. They are built to be able to stand the pressure of the water. And most of them have a swim bladder that helps them go up and down under water. This bladder is full of air. Air, of course, is lighter than water. To rise, the fish forces more air into its swim bladder. To sink, it lets some of the air out.

A submarine is streamlined. Heavy steel plates keep the pressure of the water from crushing it. It has tanks that act like a fish's swim bladder. Letting water into the tanks forces the air in them out and makes the submarine heavy enough to sink. Pumping in air forces the water out of the tanks and makes the submarine light enough to rise again.

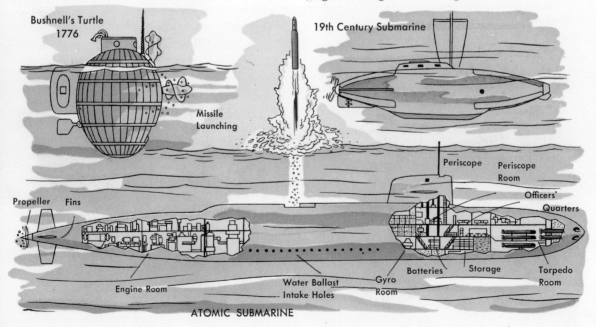

Bushnell's Turtle 1776

19th Century Submarine

Missile Launching

Periscope

Periscope Room

Officers' Quarters

Propeller   Fins

Engine Room

Water Ballast Intake Holes

Gyro Room

Batteries

Storage

Torpedo Room

ATOMIC SUBMARINE

A submarine must have something to drive it through the water. The very first underwater boat was rowed. The first good submarines used gasoline engines on the surface and electric motors under water. Later came diesel engines. Now in the newest submarines the heat from atom-splitting changes water into steam. The steam drives steam turbines.

The snorkel of a submarine is a tube for taking in air when a submarine is under water. The diving planes are a device to make the submarine dive nose first instead of sinking straight down. The periscope may be sent up when the boat is under water. Mirrors and prisms in the periscope let the men in the submarine look out over the surface of the water.

In the story Captain Nemo found underwater cruising pleasant. He even got all his food from the bottom of the sea. But people do not take trips on real submarines for fun. Submarines are built chiefly because they are useful in wartime.

The first submarine we know much about was the "Turtle." It was built by David Bushnell, a young American, during the Revolution. There was room in it for only one man. An attempt was made to carry a torpedo out in it to sink an English vessel. The "Turtle" got back safely, but the torpedo did not sink the vessel.

Not long afterward Robert Fulton, who invented the steamboat, also built a submarine. He showed it to Napoleon, but Napoleon was not interested and would not buy it. He then sold his idea to the British government. But the British government did nothing with it. Fulton's submarine was also named the "Nautilus."

The first ship ever sunk by a submarine was sunk during the War between the States. The submarine, the "Hunley," belonged to the Southern forces. The ship sunk was the Northern "Housatonic." The "Hunley," however, sank, too.

The U.S. Navy got its first submarine in 1900. In World War I and again in World War II Germany showed how important submarines can be in wartime. German U-boats destroyed a great many vessels. Building submarines is now an important way for nations to get ready to defend themselves. At the same time methods are worked out for spotting and destroying enemy submarines. (See NAVY; PERISCOPE; VERNE, JULES.)

SUBWAYS There are some problems that every big city has. One is how to keep its streets from being too crowded and too noisy. Many cities have helped to solve this problem by building subways. A subway is an underground street railway. In England subways are called tubes.

Subways are rather new. The first one was built in London about 100 years ago. It was very short. The trains were run by steam. The first subway that had electric trains, as subways have now, was built only a little more than 50 years ago. It was built in Budapest, the capital of Hungary. Boston was the first city in the United States to have a subway. Today New York has more miles of subway than any other city in the world. Moscow in the Soviet Union has the most beautiful subway stations to be found anywhere.

Of course, digging a tunnel for a subway is not easy or cheap. Keeping a subway clean and well ventilated after it is built is not easy or cheap either. But most people in the cities that have them agree that they are worth what they cost. (See CAISSON; TRANSPORTATION; TUNNELS.)

Subway trains rush along free from traffic.

The Suez Canal is a short cut to the East.

SUEZ CANAL A century ago Bombay in India was more than 12,000 miles by sea from London. Now it is only a little more than 7,000 miles. The earth, of course, is no smaller than it was. The difference is made by the Suez Canal. Ships used to have to sail around Africa to reach India from Europe. Now they can go through the Suez Canal.

This canal cuts Asia and Africa apart. It reaches from the Mediterranean Sea to the Gulf of Suez and the Red Sea. A ship going from London to Bombay sails south to the Strait of Gibraltar. It goes through the strait into the Mediterranean. It then sails the whole length of the Mediterranean till it comes to the northern end of the Suez Canal. It goes through the canal and into the Red Sea. From there it sails into the Indian Ocean and on to India.

It takes a ship less than 15 hours to sail through the canal. The canal is 103 miles long. It is twice as long as the Panama Canal and carries more than twice as much traffic. Through it is shipped about two-thirds of the oil from the Near East.

The Suez Canal goes through desert land that belongs to Egypt. There may have been a canal here in ancient days. If there was, the sand from the desert round about filled it up many centuries ago. Today's canal was not started until 1859.

The canal was built by an Egyptian company. Money for it was raised by the French, the Turks, and the Egyptians. For the first six years work was slow. Men did the digging with hand shovels. Then big machines were brought in, and the work went faster.

The canal was finished in 1869. There was a big celebration. The composer Verdi wrote the opera *Aïda* for the celebration, but it was not performed until 1871.

A few years later Britain bought many shares in the company. The route through the canal was soon so important to Britain that it was given the name "the lifeline of the British Empire." Britain built forts on lands near the canal to guard it.

It was agreed that the Suez Canal Company would collect tolls until 1968 from all ships that used the canal. But in 1956 the Egyptian government took control. Trouble between Egypt and other nations followed. The canal was blocked for many months. It was reopened early in 1957. The United Nations finally accepted Egypt's control and right to collect all tolls. Most people hope that the Suez Canal can again serve all nations.

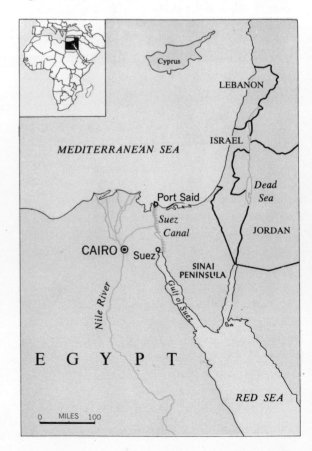

SUGAR Many fruits are sweet because they have sugar in them. Honey is sweet because it has sugar in it. Our cave-man ancestors ate fruits and honey. They therefore ate sugar. But they never saw any sugar like the sugar we buy.

The first pure sugar was produced in India about 2,000 years ago. "Sugar" comes from an Arab word. At the time of the Crusades the Arabs were using sugar for medicine and once in a while for a feast. Europeans learned about sugar from the crusaders and from the Arabs in Spain. They liked it. The trade caravans that went to the East to get spices brought back sugar, too. In time it became a common food. Today more than 50 million tons of sugar are used every year!

The sugar we buy does not come from fruit or from honey. A little of it comes from the sap of the sugar maple tree. But most of it comes from sugar cane or from sugar beets. A field of sugar cane looks much like a field of corn. Sugar beets growing look much like garden beets.

In making sugar from sugar cane, the stalks are crushed and the juice is squeezed out of them. The juice is boiled until almost all the water is driven out and it has become a thick syrup. Most of the sugar in the syrup forms into crystals. Then a machine, by whirling the mixture of crystals and syrup very fast, separates the two.

The syrup is boiled again and made into molasses. The crystals are dried. They are coarse and brown. They are called raw sugar. This raw sugar is purified and bleached to make the cane sugar we buy.

Sugar is made from sugar beets in about the same way. No one can tell from its looks or its taste whether the sugar he buys is cane sugar or beet sugar.

Sugar is good energy food. But it does not have any vitamins or minerals in it. And it does not have any body building material. The danger in eating much sugar is that it will satisfy our appetites and keep us from eating all the other foods we need.

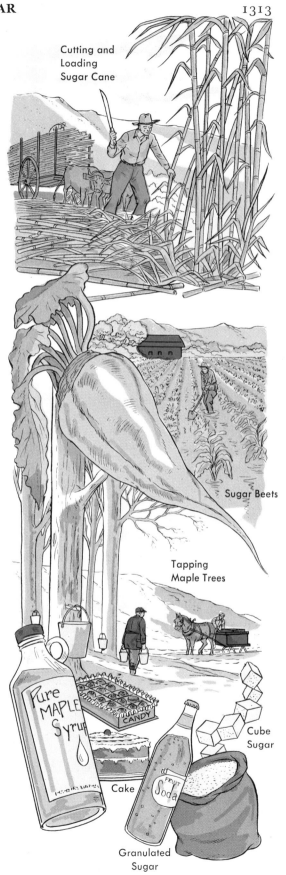

Cutting and Loading Sugar Cane

Sugar Beets

Tapping Maple Trees

Pure MAPLE Syrup

CANDY

Cake

Soda

Cube Sugar

Granulated Sugar

Sulfur melts easily.

Sulfur Crystal

Sulfur

SULFUR The earth is a great store-house. Many, many useful materials come from it. One of them is sulfur.

Sulfur can be bought in any drugstore. The sulfur one buys is always yellow, but it may be a yellow powder or yellow crystals or a hard yellow roll. In a science laboratory sulfur sometimes puts on a disguise. When heated, it sometimes changes to a brown, rubbery substance. But it never keeps this disguise long. It soon turns hard and yellow.

People have known about sulfur for thousands of years. They found out long ago that it can be set on fire easily. Another name for it is "brimstone." "Brimstone" means "burning stone."

Vesuvius is a famous volcano in Italy. Visitors to this volcano often bring away lumps of sulfur with them. The sulfur comes from the throat of the volcano. Sulfur comes from many other volcanoes, too.

But not much of our sulfur is taken from volcanoes. Most of it comes from layers of sulfur deep underground. Tons and tons of sulfur are mined every year.

Sulfur is used in medicines. It is also used in matches. But it would not take many tons for all our matches and sulfur medicines. We use far more in hardening rubber and in making sulfuric acid. Rubber is so soft and sticky that it is not very useful until sulfur is used to harden it. Sulfuric acid is used in manufacturing so many things that thousands of factories would have to shut down if this acid could not be obtained.

Sulfur is sometimes a nuisance. Sulfur fumes in the air have an unpleasant smell. One gas that is made of sulfur and hydrogen has such a bad smell that it is called "rotten egg gas." Sulfur fumes in the air cause silver to tarnish. They also make window draperies fade and rot. But on the other hand we could not live without sulfur. Our bodies must have a little of it to do their work properly. Usually we get all the sulfur we have to have in meat and eggs and cheese. (See CHEMISTRY; GOODYEAR, CHARLES; MINES AND MINING; RUBBER.)

SUN The sun is a star. It is not by any means the biggest of the stars. It looks much bigger than any other star because it is closer to us. It is only about 93,000,-000 miles away! All the other stars are much, much farther away than that.

Of course, if we were still closer to the sun it would look even bigger. If we were only a million miles away, let us say, it would fill the whole sky.

The sun is not very big as stars go, but it is enormous compared to the earth. If it were hollow, there would be room

Corona

Total Eclipse of Sun Showing Corona and Prominences

Sun Prominences Compared to Earth

Green plants use the energy that comes to them in sunlight to make food. Almost all other living things depend on green plants for food. Coal, oil, and natural gas were formed from the remains of plants and animals of long ago. In these fuels the energy of sunlight has been stored for millions of years. Scientists are now experimenting with using the sun's energy directly in solar furnaces.

Where does the sun's energy come from? Deep in its center hydrogen atoms are constantly joining to form heavier elements. Energy is constantly being produced in the process.

The spinning of the earth makes the sun rise and set and seem to move westward in the sky. The people of long ago thought that the earth stood still and that the sun moved around it. Many of them believed that each day the sun god drove the golden chariot of the sun across the sky. (See DAY AND NIGHT; ECLIPSES; SOLAR SYSTEM; STARS; SUNSPOTS; ZODIAC.)

for more than a million earths inside. This enormous ball weighs more than 300,000 times as much as the earth.

There is a great deal of talk about space travel, but no one would want to take a trip to the sun even if he could. It is so hot that no one could stand to come near it. At the center the temperature is supposed to be more than 35 million degrees!

Even if the sun were not hot, no one would dare visit it. The gravity on the surface is so great that a person would be crushed by his own weight.

The sun is far too hot to be solid. It is a huge ball of gases that are so hot that they give off light. Shooting up from the sun there are great rose-colored streamers of glowing gas. They are called solar prominences. Some of them shoot up more than 100,000 miles from the sun's surface.

The sun has a halo around it. It is called the corona. The sun's corona shows only when there is an eclipse of the sun. Scientists think that it is a cloud of very, very small particles lighted up by the main body of the sun.

We all owe our lives to the sun. If it did not send light and warmth to the earth nothing could live here. No wonder many people in ancient times worshiped it!

All our energy for useful work comes from the sun. The energy of falling water turns many of our machines. The water was first raised to the clouds as vapor by the sun's heat and then dropped as rain.

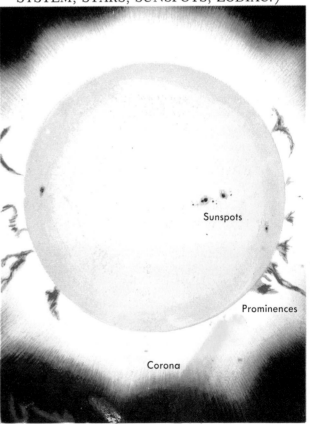
Sunspots
Prominences
Corona
The Sun—A Huge Ball of Glowing Gases

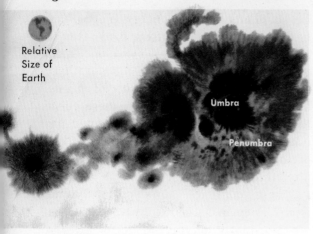

Relative Size of Earth

Umbra

Penumbra

One sunspot may be many times larger than the earth.

SUNSPOTS Great storms called sunspots sometimes rage on the surface of the sun. In pictures sunspots look dark. They are not really dark. They look dark merely because the rest of the sun is so much brighter. The darkest part of a sunspot is called the umbra. The less-dark region around it is the penumbra.

A storm on the sun may last for many days. One even lasted for 18 months. By watching sunspots scientists found out that the sun spins on its axis.

Sunspots may have something to do with our weather. They certainly sometimes interfere with radio programs.

Before the telescope was invented no one had ever seen sunspots. Galileo was probably the first person to see them. When he told about them people were not pleased. They wanted to think that the sun was perfect—a great big shining ball without a flaw. (See SOLAR SYSTEM.)

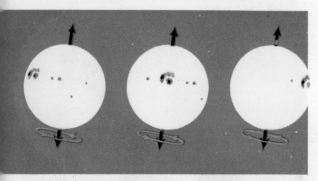

Changing position of sunspots shows the sun's rotation.

SUPERSTITIONS Many people believe that handling a toad will cause warts. Many believe that a person's future can be told from the stars. Many think that if it rains on Easter Sunday, it will rain every Sunday for the next seven weeks. There is no truth in any of these ideas. They are called superstitions.

A great many superstitions are about good luck and bad luck. The pictures on the opposite page are reminders of some of these superstitions. Finding a pin and picking it up is supposed to make the whole day go well. Friday, if it falls on the 13th of a month, is said to be an unlucky day. A four-leaved clover, a horseshoe hung up so that "the luck cannot leak out," and a rabbit's foot are a few of the things that are supposed to bring good luck. Breaking a mirror, spilling salt, walking under a ladder, having a black cat cross your path, and opening an umbrella in the house are supposed to bring bad luck.

There are many superstitions about the weather. There are many about the moon. There are many about animals. In fact, there are superstitions of some kind about almost everything around us.

Many superstitions came about from beliefs held centuries ago. No one knows how some superstitions began. Some perhaps came about because people's eyes played tricks on them. One superstition about snakes is that a snake of a certain kind can take its tail into its mouth and then roll over the ground like a hoop. Probably someone once thought that he saw a hoop snake rolling along.

There is a superstition that, if a radio announcer tells that a pitcher is pitching a no-hit baseball game, the pitcher's chances of finishing the game as a no-hit game are spoiled. It is easy to see how this superstition grew up. No-hit games are rare. A pitcher is very likely to get tired as the game goes on and give up some hits even if he did not in the early innings. If, in the middle of a game, a radio announcer says that the game is a no-hit game, the pitcher is very likely to give up a hit soon. But if he does, it is not because the announcer ruined his chances for him. He would give up the hit anyway. But it is hard to prove that the radio announcement was not the cause of the pitcher's misfortune. People would give up their superstitions more easily if it were easier to prove that there is no truth in them.

Here are some other superstitions. A few of them are common. Some of them are so silly that not many people now believe that they are true.

A blister on your tongue means that you have told a lie.

When you have cold shivers, someone is talking about you.

If you sing before breakfast, you will cry before night.

If you count your warts, make a knot in a thread for every wart, and throw the thread away, the warts will be cured.

Killing a spider is bad luck.

The seventh child of a family will always be lucky.

If you count the number of fish you have caught, you will catch no more that day.

If you hang an adder's skin in the rafters, your house will never catch fire.

BAD LUCK

Opening an Umbrella Indoors

Spilling Salt

FRIDAY 13

Breaking a Mirror

GOOD LUCK

Four-leaf Clover

Horseshoe

Black Cat

Rabbit's Foot

Walking Under a Ladder

Picking Up a Pin

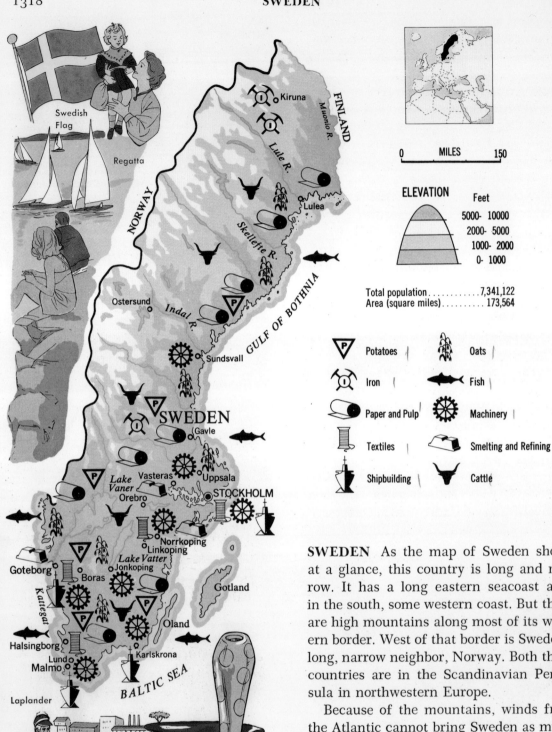

MILES 0 — 150

ELEVATION   Feet

5000- 10000
2000- 5000
1000- 2000
0- 1000

Total population...........7,341,122
Area (square miles).........173,564

Potatoes | Oats |
Iron | Fish |
Paper and Pulp | Machinery |
Textiles | Smelting and Refining
Shipbuilding | Cattle

SWEDEN As the map of Sweden shows at a glance, this country is long and narrow. It has a long eastern seacoast and, in the south, some western coast. But there are high mountains along most of its western border. West of that border is Sweden's long, narrow neighbor, Norway. Both those countries are in the Scandinavian Peninsula in northwestern Europe.

Because of the mountains, winds from the Atlantic cannot bring Sweden as much warmth as they bring to Norway's west coast in winter. In the winter, Sweden's east-coast harbors are frozen over.

There are not such good fishing grounds in the seas bordering Sweden as there are near Norway's long Atlantic coast. But in Sweden there is more room between the mountains and the sea. Much good farm-land, forest land, and iron are in the south. There are great forests and some farmland farther north. Map signs for iron near Kiruna, far to the north, show where some very rich iron ore is mined to ship abroad. And many rivers furnish water power. Sweden is prosperous.

In summer, tourists often travel on the Göta Canal across southern Sweden, in which most of the people live. Göteborg, on the west coast, and Stockholm, on the east coast, are connected by that canal as well as by road, railroad, and airline. Among things to be seen from the canal are red farmhouses and barns with white trimmings, many fields of oats and hay, other fields of food crops such as potatoes and wheat, and factories of many kinds. The oats and hay are raised to feed to dairy cows. Dairy farming is now the main kind of farming in Sweden. Much butter and many Swedish factory products are sold abroad. In the forests, logs for pulp and paper mills are cut.

Göteborg's harbor does not freeze over in winter. Stockholm's does. But icebreak-ers keep it open. Beautiful Stockholm is Sweden's largest city and the country's capital. It is built partly on islands. It is called a model city because it is very clean and has no slums. And for its modern buildings, styles were chosen which look well beside handsome ones built long ago. Among its famous buildings are the palace of the king and the beautiful Town Hall. Cutlery made of famous Swedish stainless steel and lovely Swedish-made glass can be bought in many Stockholm shops.

Sweden is a democratic kingdom. All grownups may vote. The country has en-joyed peace for almost 150 years. And to help keep Sweden prosperous, its people are learning more ways of taking good care of their valuable forests and farmlands and better and better ways of working to-gether. (See BALTIC SEA; DENMARK; FINLAND; LAPLAND; NORWAY.)

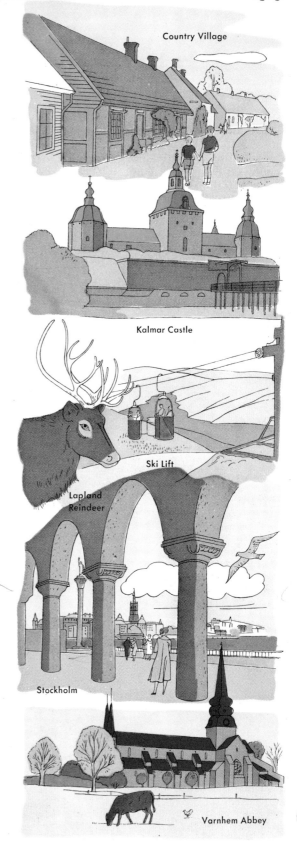

Country Village

Kalmar Castle

Lapland Reindeer

Ski Lift

Stockholm

Varnhem Abbey

Starting Position
for Racing

The Swimming Hole

SWIMMING A baby fish can swim without being taught how. So can a baby duck and a baby whale. Many other animals can, too. People are not so fortunate. They have to learn to swim. They have no fins or webbed feet or flippers to make swimming easy. But it is very much worthwhile to learn to swim for three reasons: Swimming is fun. It is good exercise for building strong bodies. And being able to swim takes away most of the danger from boating, water skiing, and other water sports.

Swimming is so popular that many public swimming pools have been built. Many public beaches have been set up. There are swimming pools in hotels, in clubhouses, in schools, and even on big ocean liners. And many families have swimming pools of their own.

Swimming is one of the sports that make up the Olympic games. Swimmers from all over the world compete in these games.

One step in learning to swim is to get over being afraid of the water. It is very encouraging to remember that our bodies, when our lungs are filled with air, are light enough to float. With practice almost everyone can learn to float on his back. A person who can float is usually no longer afraid of the water.

Another important step in learning to swim is to learn to breathe a certain way. A swimmer is supposed to breathe in through his mouth and breathe out through his nose. Of course, he must have his head

Scissors Kick

Frog Kick

Crawl

above the surface to breathe in, but he can breathe out below the surface. If a swimmer breathes as he should, he will not be in danger of getting water into his lungs.

In swimming, a person must move his arms and legs in such a way that he pushes himself along. There is more than one way of doing so. The backstroke, the crawl, the side stroke, and the butterfly stroke are four of the best-known ways. The pictures show these different strokes.

Swimming is never as fast as running. But the best swimmers can swim fast. For instance, the record for the men's backstroke for 100 yards is 55-7/10 seconds.

Some swimmers pride themselves on being able to swim long distances. Swimming the English Channel is one of the long distance tests. The Channel, at the place where swimmers usually try it, is about 20 miles wide. In the past 50 years more than 60 swimmers have succeeded in swimming across it. In 1875 Matthew Webb, of Britain, swam from England to France in 21 hours and 45 minutes. In 1955 Florence Chadwick, an American, swam the same distance in 13 hours and 55 minutes. Because of the tides in the Channel, better time has been made in the other direction. In 1950 Hassan Abd el Rehim, an Egyptian, swam from France to England in 10 hours and 49 minutes.

Many swimmers are interested in diving. Skin diving is now becoming very popular. (See DIVING; SKIN DIVING.)

Butterfly Stroke

Start

Finish

Side Stroke

Back Float

Backstroke

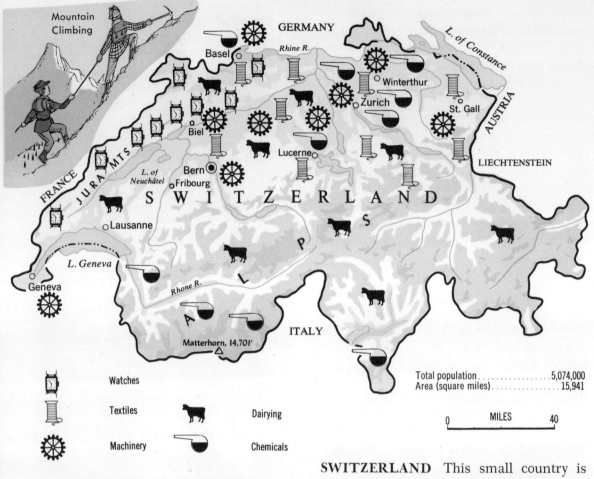

Mountain Climbing

FRANCE
JURA MTS
Basel
Biel
L. of Neuchâtel
Bern
Fribourg
Lausanne
L. Geneva
Geneva
GERMANY
Rhine R.
Winterthur
Zurich
St. Gall
Lucerne
S W I T Z E R L A N D
L. of Constance
AUSTRIA
LIECHTENSTEIN
A L P S
Rhone R.
Matterhorn, 14,701'
ITALY

Total population................5,074,000
Area (square miles)...............15,941

0   MILES   40

Watches

Textiles   Dairying

Machinery   Chemicals

ELEVATION Feet

Over 10000
5000- 10000
2000- 5000
1000- 2000
0- 1000

Ski Lift in the Alps

SWITZERLAND This small country is in western central Europe. As the map shows, little Switzerland is mountainous. It is surrounded by France, Germany, Austria, and Italy. The Swiss do not have a language of their own. Many speak German. The others speak French or Italian.

Switzerland is poor in minerals. It has long cold winters and cool summers. All year round, snow covers some of its mountain peaks. Much land cannot be plowed. But the Swiss make good livings. Little Switzerland is prosperous.

About a fifth of the Swiss are farmers. Most of them, as the map suggests, have a few dairy cows. In the Alps Mountains in southern Switzerland, there are many high valleys. Very high up on many mountain slopes are small pastures where cows can graze in summer. While their cows are in such pastures, farmers raise hay for winter feed for them on lower valley-side slopes. Near valley homes, the farmers plow a little land and raise vegetables and fruits for their own use. They sell milk and cheese. In the hilly plateau north of the Alps we see larger fields of crops on the flatter land and many pastures and cows in hilly land.

In that plateau there are lovely lakes and lakeside cities, too. Zurich is the largest city. Bern is the Swiss capital. There are many more factory workers in Switzerland than there are farmers. Most factories are in the cities. The map shows four of the main kinds of factory products. Cheese and milk chocolate are famous products, too. Swift streams help produce electricity for the factories.

The biggest business in Switzerland is the tourist industry. Each year, by bus, automobile, train, airplane, or river boat, about a million visitors come to Switzerland. A few come on bicycles. There is skiing for winter visitors. But most tourists want to see beautiful Switzerland in the summertime.

The Swiss have done much to help to attract tourists. Their many hotels are famous for good service. The people have worked hard to make travel from place to place pleasant and speedy. All trains are electric trains. Roads, railroads, bridges, and tunnels have been built in many places where such things are very hard to build. By auto or bus, we can go very close to the great Rhone glacier. On a special kind of aerial railway, called a funicular railway, trains take people up very steep slopes. From these slopes they can see clearly such great peaks as the Matterhorn.

Mountains have helped to protect the Swiss from invaders. In many European wars, little Switzerland has remained "an island of peace." After World War I, a beautiful palace was built in the city of Geneva for the League of Nations. Now this famous palace is used by some agencies of the United Nations. (See ALPS; CHEESE; CLOCKS AND WATCHES.)

Swiss Flag

Alps

Skiing

Monk and St. Bernard Dog

Swiss Chalet

Village Street

Watchmaking

Cheese Production

Alpine Flower

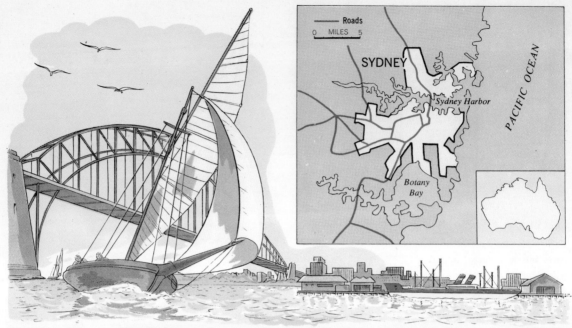

Pleasure boats and ocean-going ships find shelter in Sydney Harbor.

SYDNEY More than half of all the people of Australia live in cities. The largest of these cities is Sydney. About two million people live there.

Sydney is the capital of the state of New South Wales. This state is in the southeastern part of Australia.

The city is on the south shore of a long, deep bay called Port Jackson. The first English settlement in New South Wales was on Botany Bay, a little south of Port Jackson. From this first settlement men went exploring to find a better place for a city. They chose the place where Sydney now is. They picked this place because there was a good spring of water near by and because big ships could come close to shore. Their choice was a good one. All Australians are proud of the beauty of Sydney's harbor. Up from the edge of the blue waters of the huge bay rise the buildings of the city. Many of these buildings are partly hidden by trees.

Today the harbor is a very busy place. Vessels from all over the world come to the docks at Sydney. They bring oil from the Near East, tobacco from the Carolinas in the United States, cloth, drugs, fertiliz-ers, and other products. From the grain elevators on the waterfront wheat is poured into the holds of freighters bound for Britain. Refrigerator ships take on butter, cheese, and meat. Other ships carry wool and lumber. Of course, most of these cargoes come from the region around Sydney. Roads and railroads reach Sydney from north, south, and west. Many of them have to cross the Blue Mountains to reach the city.

Sydney looks much like an American city. There are many office buildings, stores, and factories. But there are no very tall buildings. Many newcomers to Australia find work in the flour mills, sugar refineries, automobile factories, and meat-freezing plants. One of the world's great bridges crosses the bay from Sydney to North Sydney. The steelwork for "Harbour Bridge" was made in Sydney's own steel mills. Many workers cross this bridge on their way from the suburbs as they go to their work in Sydney.

The city has pleasant parks and beautiful homes. At least 20 good beaches help give Sydney playgrounds for its many people and visitors to enjoy.

The letter *T* was first a cross (+). Today if a person cannot sign his name, he makes a cross. The same mark was used long ago. The inventors of the alphabet called the mark a "taw" and used it to stand for the sound of *T*. In the Phoenician alphabet it was turned on its side (X). The Greeks stood it up again and took off the top (T). It came down to us by way of the Romans.

T usually stands for the sound it has in *top* and *potato*. It has a different sound in *question*. In *listen* and some other words it is silent.

TAILORBIRD Some kinds of birds build very strange nests. Among the most curious of all birds' nests are those made by tailorbirds. These small songbirds actually sew their nests together.

The tailorbird is able to use its thin sharp bill as a needle. It takes bits of grass or vegetable fiber or even of spider web to use as thread. To make its nest, the bird sews large leaves together in the shape of a

Tailorbird

snug pocket. Then it makes a comfortable lining in this pocket by putting wool or fine hair or more grass in it. The female tailorbird usually lays three or four pinkish or greenish eggs at a time.

Tailorbirds are found in India, Ceylon, Malaya, southern China, and the Philippine Islands. They belong to the large warbler group. Although they cannot compare in beauty with such oriental birds as the peacock, tailorbirds are very attractive. They have olive-green backs and pale yellowish stomachs. The crowns of their heads are chestnut-colored.

TAJ MAHAL One of the sights of India is the tomb of the emperor Shah Jehan and his favorite queen. The tomb is the Taj Mahal. Many people think that it is the most beautiful building in the whole world. Its name means "gem of buildings."

The Taj Mahal is in Agra, India. It was built between three and four centuries ago.

A legend tells that the queen, who was called Mumtaz-i-Mahal, first saw this building in a dream. She saw it so clearly that she remembered it after she wakened. She told the emperor about it, and he set to work at once to have it built. No one knows whether the story of the dream is true. We do know that an army of workmen spent 22 years in building the Taj Mahal. We

know, too, that it cost many millions of dollars to build.

The tomb is tall. The tip of the dome reaches as high as an 18-story building. The whole building is of white marble. In places the marble has been carved so that it looks like lace. Inside there is much carving. There is more of the marble lace. In addition, parts of the Koran, the sacred book of the Moslems, have been carved on the walls. In other places the walls are covered with flower designs. Colored stones such as jasper and carnelian are set in the white stone.

The building would not be so beautiful if it were not in such a beautiful setting. Much of the ground around it is paved with red sandstone. There are pools of quiet water that reflect the dome and the slender towers. Round about there is a beautiful garden. The Taj Mahal is worth going a long way to see. (See ARCHITECTURE; INDIA; ISLAM.)

TAPESTRY   The castles of the Middle Ages were dark and gloomy. The inside walls as well as the outside walls were stone. They were not plastered or painted or papered. But the walls of some rooms were lovely because they were hung with pieces of woven cloth called tapestries. There were tapestries in cathedrals, too.

All medieval tapestries had pictures or designs woven into them. Many of the pictures told interesting stories. One famous tapestry—the Bayeux tapestry—shows King Harold of England being told about the landing of William the Conqueror. Halley's comet, which was visible at the time, is shown in the tapestry. The people of those days thought that a comet was a warning of some disaster. In some cases it took several tapestries to tell a story. A famous set of tapestries is called "The Lady and the Unicorn." It is now one of the treasures of the Cluny Museum in Paris.

Tapestries were made mostly of wool or linen, but threads of silk might be woven in. Gold threads were sometimes used, too.

Tapestries were being made in Egypt at least 3,000 years ago. They were also made in other ancient countries. The finest tapestries of the Middle Ages were woven in France and Flanders.

In modern times tapestry making almost died out. But people are interested in it once more. Some beautiful tapestries are now being made. (See CASTLES; CATHEDRALS; MIDDLE AGES; SPINNING AND WEAVING.)

American Craftsmen's Council
"Unicorn" by Mark Adams

Detail of "The Last Supper" by Raphael   *Leeser-Camera Clix*

Here are two outstanding examples of Renaissance and modern tapestry designs. Raphael's masterpiece is sixteenth century, and Adams' "Unicorn" is twentieth century.

The little tarsier has large owl-like eyes.

TARSIER The tarsier is a relative of the monkeys and the lemurs. Tarsiers are little animals—when full grown they are no bigger than rats. They are found in the East Indies and on some of the other islands in the Pacific Ocean.

The most noticeable things about tarsiers are their big eyes, their long, thin tails, their long hind legs, and their long fingers and toes. On their fingers and toes they have pads like those of tree toads. These pads help them as they climb about in their tree homes.

Tarsiers eat lizards and insects. As their big owl-like eyes suggest, tarsiers do their hunting at night. (See MONKEYS.)

TATTOOING The decorations on the skin of the people in the picture will not wash off. They are tattooed on. Tattooing is done as a rule by pricking deep holes in the skin and putting colored dyes in them. Or it may be done in a way that is much like sewing. Colored threads are drawn through the skin. They leave color behind them. There is no easy way for a person to remove a tattoo.

Tattooing is very old. From Egyptian mummies we find that some of the ancient Egyptians decorated themselves in this way. It was once common in many parts of the world. It is still common among some tribes of Africa and the Pacific Islands. And sailors of many lands through-out the world still think it is "the thing to do" to have themselves tattooed.

Tattooing is painful. It is not easy to see how people came to use that way of decorating themselves. Perhaps the very fact that it is painful is one reason that it came to be used. A man could show that he was brave and could stand pain by having himself tattooed. Besides, among many peoples tattoos came to be much more than a decoration. A tattoo could be used to show to what tribe a person belonged. Some tattoos had a religious meaning. And warriors found that if their faces were tattooed no one could tell from their expressions whether they were frightened. Fortunately, as tribes have become civilized, they have used tattooing less. (See SAVAGES.)

Melanesian

Egyptian

Japanese

Australian

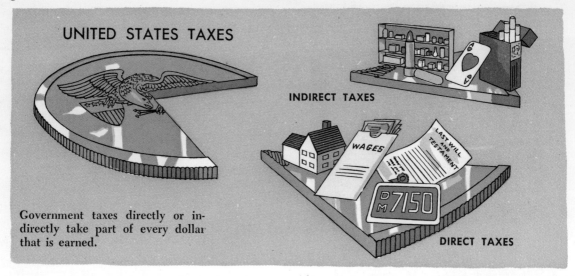

UNITED STATES TAXES

INDIRECT TAXES

WAGES

LAST WILL AND TESTAMENT

PM 7150

DIRECT TAXES

Government taxes directly or indirectly take part of every dollar that is earned.

TAXES Today we ask our governments to do many things for us. We want soldiers, sailors, and policemen to protect us. We want good roads and well-lighted streets. We want our mail carried, and our sewage and garbage taken away. We want fires fought and quarrels settled and people without work helped. We want good schools and hospitals. This is just the beginning of a very long list of what we ask our governments to do.

To do all that we ask, governments have to have money. A government has no magic way of getting people to work for it and of getting the materials it needs. It must pay for both work and materials. Most of the money the governments of today spend comes from taxes—from money that they collect from their people. They collect some of their taxes from individuals, some from corporations.

Is there no better way for a government to get the money it needs than by collecting taxes? It is true that at times governments have tried other ways. The "robber barons" of the Middle Ages carried on raids on one another and on the towns. They also robbed travelers that passed through their lands. The ancient Romans and many later nations conquered other people and took great sums of gold and silver from them. The early Spanish explorers

took back from the New World great stores of gold and silver from the Indian nations they conquered. Fortunately most people have outgrown the idea of paying government expenses by raids and conquest.

Another very old idea was that governments should be supported by slave labor. Much of the work of the governments in ancient Greece, for example, was done by slaves. Some of the ancient Greeks went so far as to say that taxes were a disgrace. We think that slavery is a disgrace today.

Many of the kings of earlier times got part of the money they needed from buried treasure. In the days of pirates, large sums were often found. Now such treasure amounts to very little.

Governments print the paper money we use. Couldn't they just print enough money to pay for what they need? Some governments have really tried printing all the money they needed. Early in the history of the United States the Continental Congress printed a great deal of money when they had nothing in the treasury to back the money. Soon the paper money was worth so little that "not worth a Continental" meant "worth less than nothing."

None of these ways is a good substitute for taxes. A government, however, does not have to get all its money from taxes. Almost every government gets some gifts, and most governments collect some fines from people who have broken the law. Almost every government charges for some of the work it does. The United States Government, for example, sells postage stamps to help pay the cost of carrying the mail. Some governments still have land to sell. But most of the money for the work of a government comes from taxes.

There are a great many kinds of taxes. Property taxes, income taxes, inheritance taxes, and sales taxes are a few of them. It is fairer to the people of a country, most people think, to have many kinds of taxes than to depend on only one kind.

Almost everyone agrees that those should pay most in taxes who can afford to

STATE TAXES ARE USED FOR:

Libraries · Social Services · Schools · STATE POLICE · Law Enforcement · Roads

pay most. Governments, therefore, ask people with big incomes, and owners of valuable property, and those who inherit big sums of money to pay more than those who have less to pay with. This plan is not followed with every kind of tax. In the case of a sales tax everybody pays the same tax on the same article.

Most people pay more in taxes than they know they do. For some taxes are hidden. The price of something one buys may include many different taxes. No one can tell, for instance, what part of the taxes of the grocer, the baker, the miller, and the farmer is hidden in the price of a loaf of bread. Taxes included in prices of things we buy are often called indirect taxes.

Some of the taxes of the past have had bad effects. Almost 300 years ago, for example, a tax on windows was levied in England. The more windows a man had

FEDERAL TAXES ARE USED FOR:

Defense · HIGHWAY BILL · SOCIAL SECURITY · Agriculture · Congress · Government Agencies

in his house, the more he was supposed to be able to pay in taxes. To cut down their taxes people began walling up their windows. New houses were built with almost no windows at all. The people who plan taxes must think about the possible bad effects of the taxes.

Taxes of today are paid in money. But they have not always been. The ancient Egyptians brought to their treasury such things as grain, cattle, honey, wine, and linen. The early Chinese emperors collected salt, jade, rice, rattan, and wild silk. Many of the early Moslems paid taxes in camels and goats.

In early days, too, many people paid taxes in labor. In China, when the Great Wall was being built, the emperor demanded a tax of three months' labor from every man. Of course, collecting taxes in goods and labor has been given up.

Many people complain about the taxes they have to pay. And probably no government has ever been able to set up a system of taxes that was fair to everyone. But giving up the services taxes pay for would certainly set civilization back thousands of years. (See GOVERNMENT; MIDDLE AGES; MONEY; SLAVERY.)

LOCAL TAXES ARE USED FOR:

Education · Water · MEN AT WORK · Police and Fire Departments · Maintenance

TEA In the United States tea is not as popular as coffee. But in many parts of the world tea is better liked. And even Americans buy millions of pounds a year.

Tea had an important part in the early story of the United States. The colonists did not like the tax England forced them to pay on tea. At the famous Boston Tea Party some of them dressed as Indians and boarded three ships which were loaded with tea. They dumped all the tea into the harbor. The Boston Tea Party helped bring on the Revolutionary War.

A pound of tea is made of hundreds of dried tea leaves. The plant they come from is a small evergreen tree. Usually on a tea plantation the trees are trimmed so that they are only about three feet tall.

When they are three years old the trees are ready for the first picking. Only the buds and the very young leaves are picked. Pickers with baskets walk along the rows, breaking off the buds and leaves. Picking is done several times a season.

JAPANESE AND CHINESE TEA PROCESSING

Tea Leaves

Curing Tea by Steaming Over Charcoal

Drying Tea by Basket Firing

Separating Dried Tea Leaves

U.S.A.

Packaged Tea

There are many kinds of tea. But most of them can be classed as either green tea or black tea. The leaves for them are the same. The difference is in the way the leaves are treated after they are picked.

The leaves for black tea are spread out on trays to wilt for a day or two. Then they are crushed between rollers. Again they are spread out. They now ferment. Their color and flavor change. When the fermenting has gone on long enough, it is stopped by heating the leaves. The leaves are rolled once more and are put in a firing room, where hot air dries them. They are now ready to be sorted, packed, and shipped.

Green tea is simply unfermented tea. The leaves are rolled and fired without being allowed to ferment.

Tea leaves take up other odors and flavors easily. Teas with special odors and flavors can be bought. To make jasmine tea, jasmine flowers are spread over the tea leaves as they are being dried.

Tea is raised in many parts of the Far East. Drinking tea is a very old custom there. Tea reached Europe for the first time about 300 years ago.

People who like tea often have their special way of making it. Most English people, instead of making a cup of tea with a tea bag, brew it by pouring hot water over loose tea leaves. (See COFFEE.)

TEETH "Scarcer than hens' teeth" means none at all, for hens have no teeth. No birds have teeth. But many animals besides ourselves do have. Snakes have teeth with very sharp points. Poisonous snakes have special teeth called fangs. Many kinds of fish have teeth. Nearly all mammals have teeth.

Squirrels, beavers, gophers, mice, and all the rodents have two very sharp teeth in the front of each jaw. They use their teeth to gnaw with. Beavers cut down trees, squirrels open nuts, and gophers gnaw grain. The cat and all its cousins have tearing teeth. They use them to tear meat.

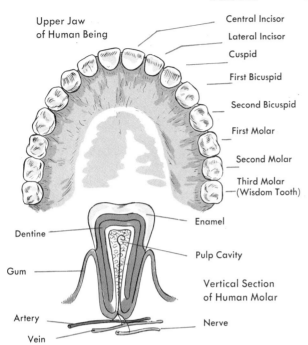

Upper Jaw of Human Being

Central Incisor
Lateral Incisor
Cuspid
First Bicuspid
Second Bicuspid
First Molar
Second Molar
Third Molar (Wisdom Tooth)

Dentine

Gum

Artery

Vein

Enamel

Pulp Cavity

Vertical Section of Human Molar

Nerve

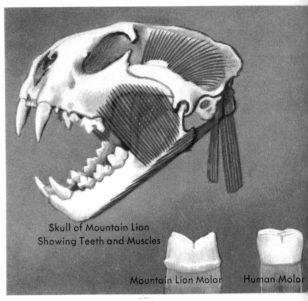

Skull of Mountain Lion Showing Teeth and Muscles

Mountain Lion Molar   Human Molar

All members of the dog family have tearing teeth, too. Horses and cows have cutting and grinding teeth. In the front of their jaws are teeth with which they cut grass. On each side are grinding teeth.

People eat both meat and plant foods. They have cutting, tearing, and grinding teeth. The diagram shows the teeth in the upper jaw. In the lower jaw there are teeth that match these.

A person has two sets of teeth. His 20 baby or "milk" teeth begin coming in when he is about six months old. He begins to lose them at about the age of six years. Permanent teeth come in as he loses his baby teeth. There are 32 permanent teeth. The last four, the wisdom teeth, may not come in for 14 or 15 years.

Part of every tooth is hidden in the jaw. This part is the root. The part that shows is the crown. The crown is covered with enamel, the hardest material in the human body. Inside the enamel is a softer material called dentine. In the very center of the tooth is the pulp cavity. Blood vessels and nerves are found in the pulp cavity.

Our teeth help us chew our food and prepare it for digestion. They also help us talk. We make some sounds, such as *th* and *v*, with the help of our teeth. Besides, our teeth help give shape to our faces.

Keeping teeth clean is very important. Brushing regularly helps to take small bits of food away from the teeth. If bits of food are never left between the teeth, tooth decay is much less likely to occur. Regular trips to the dentist are very wise. A dentist can help keep the teeth clean and can find cavities before they become large. (See BODY, HUMAN; DENTISTRY.)

TELEGRAPH Electricity travels amazingly fast. It makes a wonderful messenger. The telegraph is the oldest way of using it as a messenger.

The word "telegraph" means "write far away." The first telegraph receivers did write out the message. They wrote it in dots and dashes on a moving strip of paper. Later, the telegraph operators found that they could receive messages faster by listening to the dots and dashes.

The telegraph sending key shown in the picture is the kind that was used for many years and is still seen occasionally. When the key is held down, it permits electricity to flow to the receiver, or sounder. When the key is released and springs up, the electricity stops flowing.

The most important parts of a telegraph sounder are an electromagnet and an iron bar. When a current of electricity flows through the coils of the electromagnet, the magnet pulls the iron bar down. When the current stops flowing, the magnet ceases to attract the iron bar and a spring forces the bar back up. The bar is mounted in a frame in such a way that when it moves down it makes a click. It makes another click when it flies up. For a dot the key is held down for a very short time. The downward click and the upward click of the iron bar come very close together. For a dash the key is held down a longer time. The clicks are farther apart.

The first message over the first telegraph line was sent May 24, 1844. The message traveled a little over 40 miles from Baltimore to Washington, D.C. Now, not much more than 100 years later, several million miles of telegraph lines are in use.

Almost as soon as the telegraph was invented, scientists began looking for ways of cutting down the amount of wire needed. Wire is expensive, and there is the additional cost of stringing it from poles or laying it underground. Scientists soon discovered that, instead of having to use two wires for a complete telegraph circuit between a sender and a receiver, it is possible to use the ground as one wire. Then they found ways of sending two, then four, and then many messages over one wire at the same time. They even found ways of sending messages in both directions over a wire at one time. Now still another way has been found of reducing the number of wires. In many places telegraph messages go part of the way by radio waves.

Many improvements have been made in ways of sending and receiving telegraph messages. Teletype machines are used in many offices today. With some teletype machines the operator types the message to be sent on a special typewriter that punches holes in a tape. The tape then goes through a sending machine, or automatic transmitter. More than 300 words a minute can be sent in this way. The teletype machine that receives the message types it out in regular letters. The telegraph is again true to its name of "writing far away." Teletype machines are now found not only in telegraph offices, but also in many newspapers and business offices.

It is now even possible to send pictures over telegraph wires. Special machines which are called facsimile (fack SIM i lee) machines are used for telegraphing pictures from one place to another. These machines are used for sending news pictures around the world. (See MAGNETS; MORSE, SAMUEL F. B.; SIGNALING.)

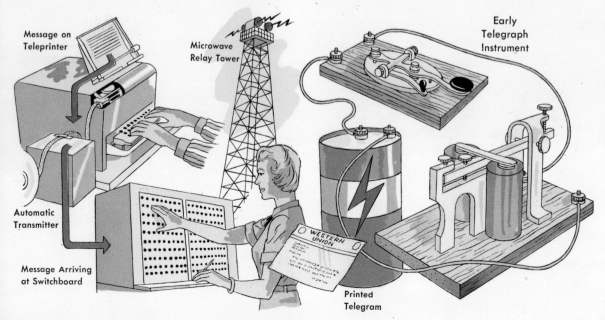

Message on Teleprinter

Microwave Relay Tower

Early Telegraph Instrument

Automatic Transmitter

Message Arriving at Switchboard

WESTERN UNION

Printed Telegram

TELEPHONE The telegraph, which was invented in 1837, proved that electricity is a wonderful messenger. But early telegraph messages had to be sent in code. Very soon people began asking, "Isn't there some way of making electricity carry spoken words, too?"

Sound travels faster and farther in some materials than in air. But sound does not travel well enough in any material we know of to make sound itself a good messenger for long distances.

In 1876 Alexander Graham Bell found a way of making sounds produce changes in a current of electricity flowing through a wire. And he found a way of using these changes to produce sound. He invented the telephone. "Telephone" comes from the Greek words meaning "speak far away."

The diagram at the top of the next column shows a very simple telephone circuit. A transmitter is connected with a receiver. A current from a cell flows through them.

A carbon chamber, which contains grains of carbon, is the heart of the transmitter. The current flows in by one wire, passes through the carbon chamber, and flows out by the other wire.

At the front of the carbon chamber is a thin metal disk called a diaphragm. As a person talks into the transmitter, sound waves make the diaphragm vibrate, or move back and forth. When the diaphragm pushes in, it presses the carbon grains closer together. When it moves out, the carbon grains move farther apart. A stronger current flows through the carbon chamber when the grains are close together than when they are farther apart.

In the telephone receiver there is an electromagnet. There is also a diaphragm. The current of electricity flows through the coils of the electromagnet. The stronger the current is, the stronger the magnet is. When the magnet is strong, it pulls hard on the diaphragm and bends it nearer to the magnet. When the magnet is weak, the diaphragm springs back.

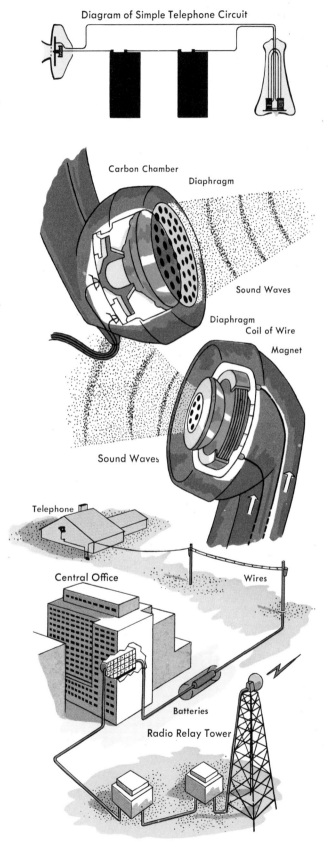

Diagram of Simple Telephone Circuit

Carbon Chamber

Diaphragm

Sound Waves

Diaphragm

Coil of Wire

Magnet

Sound Waves

Telephone

Central Office

Wires

Batteries

Radio Relay Tower

The changing current actually makes the diaphragm in the receiver move back and forth just as the diaphragm in the transmitter is moving. As the receiver diaphragm moves back and forth, it produces sound waves like those made by the person talking into the transmitter.

Of course, actual telephone circuits are much more complicated than the one in the diagram. At each end of a line there must be a transmitter, a receiver, and some signal such as a bell. Besides, a person who has a telephone wants to be able to talk with a great many other people who have telephones. There must be telephone exchanges where connections are made. These connections may be made at a switchboard by a telephone operator. With modern dial telephones the connections are made automatically.

Over long distances telephone calls may go part of the way by radio relay. And now undersea telephone cables let us talk to people an ocean away almost as easily as to someone in the next block. (See BELL, ALEXANDER GRAHAM; ELECTRICITY.)

TELESCOPE In 1609 Galileo, the famous Italian scientist, heard that a Dutch spectacle-maker had invented a new kind of instrument. With it he could make things faraway appear to be close.

The Dutch spectacle-maker, most accounts say, was Hans Lippershey. One story tells that a boy who was learning the trade from Lippershey was playing with some of the lenses Lippershey used for spectacles. He happened to hold one in front of another and look through them. To his surprise the lenses seemed to bring what he was looking at much closer. He showed Lippershey his discovery.

Lippershey put the two lenses in a tube. He put the new toy in his shop window. It was, of course, a simple telescope. The word "telescope" means "seeing far away."

As soon as he heard of a telescope, Galileo decided to make one for himself. With

Lippershey made a simple telescope.

the first telescope he made Galileo found that he could sight vessels too far out at sea to be seen with the naked eye.

Galileo soon made better telescopes than his first one. When he finished his fourth telescope, it occurred to him to look up at the sky with it. He turned it toward the moon, and had a great surprise. The moon was not a smooth, shining ball as people had said. Instead, it had mountains and valleys and plains on it.

Ever since that time telescopes have been used to explore the sky. There are still small telescopes for seeing distant things on the earth. But the famous telescopes have all been built to study the sky.

Galileo's telescopes were made with two small lenses. Some of the best telescopes in the world are still made with lenses. Telescopes made with lenses are called refracting telescopes.

The world's largest refracting telescope is in Yerkes Observatory at Williams Bay, Wis. The biggest lens in this telescope is 40 inches across.

Not long after Galileo's time the famous English scientist Newton invented another kind of telescope. In it he used mirrors instead of lenses. Telescopes made with mirrors are called reflecting telescopes.

The biggest reflecting telescope in the world is the Hale telescope in the observatory on Mount Palomar in California. It has been called the "giant of Palomar."

The big mirror in this telescope is 200 inches across—nearly 17 feet. The mirror is made of glass with a thin coating of aluminum. It weighs nearly 15 tons. The whole telescope weighs more than 500 tons. It is 6 stories tall. Building it took 20 years and cost 8 million dollars.

Many problems had to be solved in building this giant telescope. Making a mirror 200 inches across was one of the hardest tasks. At first the plan was to make the mirror of pure quartz. But that plan was given up. The mirror was made of Pyrex glass instead. After the molten glass was poured it had to be left in the mold for a whole year to cool.

Then came the problem of taking it from Corning, N. Y., where it was made, to California. A special car was built for it. The train had to go to California by a roundabout way to avoid all low bridges and narrow tunnels. It made the trip to Los Angeles safely. There workmen began the work of polishing the mirror.

The polishing went on for 11½ years. At the beginning the mirror weighed about 20 tons. Five tons of glass were polished away. At last, late in 1947, the mirror was taken up the mountain by truck. Several bridges had to be strengthened before it was allowed to cross them. For part of the way tractors helped by pushing and pull-

Reflecting Telescope — Mount Palomar California

ing. Everyone was greatly relieved when the mirror reached its mountaintop without any mishap.

While the mirror was being polished, an observatory to hold the telescope and the telescope's framework were built. The dome of the observatory is air-conditioned. The machinery that turns the telescope is very delicate. A change in temperature might undo days of work. There is a special room for visitors. A glass wall prevents heat from their bodies from reaching the telescope. Big as the telescope is, it can

Diagram of a Refracting Telescope

The largest reflecting telescope in the world is in this observatory in California on Mount Palomar. Its large reflector, or mirror, is 200 inches, or almost 17 feet, across.

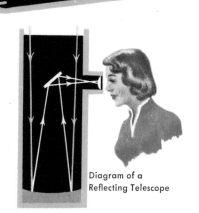

Diagram of a Reflecting Telescope

Television Studio

Engineering Control Room

Actors

2

TV Camera

be moved easily so that it will point to exactly the right place in the sky. The electric motor in an ordinary washing machine would be strong enough to move it.

It is possible for an astronomer to study the sky by looking through the world's biggest telescopes. But scientists have found a better way of making discoveries with them. A photographic plate is a better "eye" than a real eye. Astronomers therefore use the telescopes as giant cameras. They take pictures of the part of the sky they wish to study and then study the pictures.

With the giant telescope of Palomar astronomers have been able to explore farther into space than ever before. They have seen great star cities a billion light-years away. These cities are, that is, so far away that the light that reaches the telescope left the stars a billion years ago! (See STARS; UNIVERSE.)

TELEVISION The word "television" comes from the Greek word that means "far away" and the Latin word that means "see." But television is not only seeing far away; it is hearing far away, too. It is radio with pictures added.

The pictures of television, like the sounds of radio, do not themselves travel through the air. At the broadcasting station both the pictures and the sounds are changed into invisible waves. In the receiving set the waves are changed back into pictures and sounds.

The "seeing" part of a television camera is an electron tube called an Orthicon tube. Light enters this tube through a lens and is focused on a light-sensitive screen. When the light strikes this screen it causes electrons to be knocked out of it. More electrons are knocked out where the light is strong than where the light is dim. The electrons flow to a plate called the target. They make an invisible electron picture on the target plate.

The picture is now changed into a current called the picture signal which flows to the transmitter. On its way the current is strengthened, or amplified.

But the whole picture cannot be changed into a picture signal at the same time. It must be changed bit by bit. At the back end of the Orthicon tube is an electron gun. This gun "scans" the electron picture on the target. It sweeps across the target in straight lines, just as we read line after line of type on a page. It goes across the target 525 times at each scanning, and then it starts over again. It covers the entire target 30 times every second! Some of the electrons the gun shoots out bounce back. More bounce back from some parts of the picture than from others. The stream of electrons bouncing back form a varying current, which becomes the picture signal.

While the pictures are being changed into picture signals, the sounds are being changed into sound signals. The transmitter sends both these signals out into space.

Children Watching TV at Home

How signals are broadcast is described in the article on RADIO.

The important part of a television receiver is a cathode-ray tube, or picture tube. At the back of this tube there is an electron gun like the one in the camera. It sweeps back and forth across the picture tube in exact timing with the gun in the camera. The gun shoots out a beam of electrons that varies just as the beam bounced back from the target in the camera varies. The big end of the picture tube—the screen we look at—is coated inside with a chemical that glows when electrons strike it.

As the electrons strike one bit after another of the screen, they create the same picture the camera "sees." The pictures follow one another so fast that they are like moving pictures. At the same time that the picture tube is forming its picture, other tubes and a loudspeaker are producing the sounds that come from the set.

The waves that carry TV programs travel out in straight lines from the broadcasting station. Since the earth is curved, a television receiving set will not work if it is very far from a sending station. At a distance of only 100 miles, one needs a very tall aerial to pick up the waves.

Color television is, of course, more complicated than black-and-white television. But the general plan is the same; pictures are changed into invisible waves that are changed back into pictures. (See ELECTRONICS; MOTION PICTURES; RADIO.)

TEN COMMANDMENTS The Bible tells us that God gave the Ten Commandments to Moses at the top of Mount Sinai. Moses was leading the Hebrews out of Egypt, where they had been captives, back to their homeland. While Moses was receiving the Ten Commandments from God, the Bible story tells, there was much lightning. The noise of thunder mingled with the sound of trumpets.

Many people think that the story of the Ten Commandments is not true word for word. They think that it is just a way of saying that God gave Moses the inspiration for the Commandments. But millions and millions of people agree that the Commandments are good rules to live by.

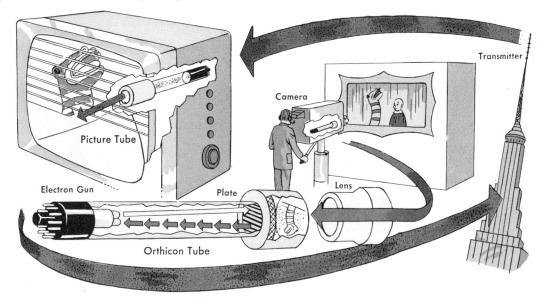
Transmitter
Camera
Lens
Picture Tube
Electron Gun
Plate
Orthicon Tube

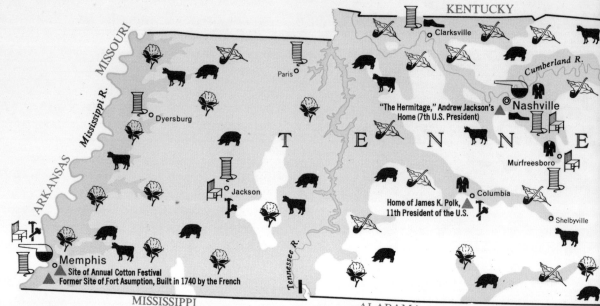

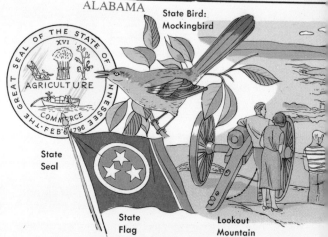

State Bird: Mockingbird

State Seal

State Flag

Lookout Mountain

TENNESSEE This southeastern state stretches westward to the Mississippi River from the Appalachians. Its width from east to west is four times its length from north to south. Tennessee was probably named after an ancient capital of the Cherokee Indians. One of its nicknames is "Volunteer State." In every war since the Revolutionary War, more Tennessee men have volunteered than the government asked for.

The earliest white settlers in Tennessee came from Virginia and North Carolina. They settled in the eastern mountains in 1769. In 1779 a band of pioneers came farther into Tennessee by way of the Cumberland Gap and the "Wilderness Road." They built Fort Nashborough near the Cumberland River in the heart of the fertile bluegrass region. This fortified settlement was the beginning of Nashville.

After the Revolutionary War, thousands of eastern families and war veterans poured into Tennessee. In 1796 it became the 16th state of the Union. The capital is Nashville. Tennessee is not a large state, but it is rather thickly settled. The number of people living in cities is less than the number on farms and in small villages.

Tennessee, however, has four cities that have over 100,000 people each.

Early settlers spoke of three very different regions in Tennessee. "The East" is mountain and plateau country. The Great Smoky Mountains are one of the nation's most beautiful vacation areas. The rugged Cumberland Plateau is mining country, rich in coal and other minerals. Between the mountains and the plateau lies the Great Valley, which is rich in fertile crop lands and apple orchards.

"The Middle" contains great bluegrass meadows, and fields of corn, hay, and tobacco. Its farms are famous for purebred horses, dairy cows, beef cattle, and hogs.

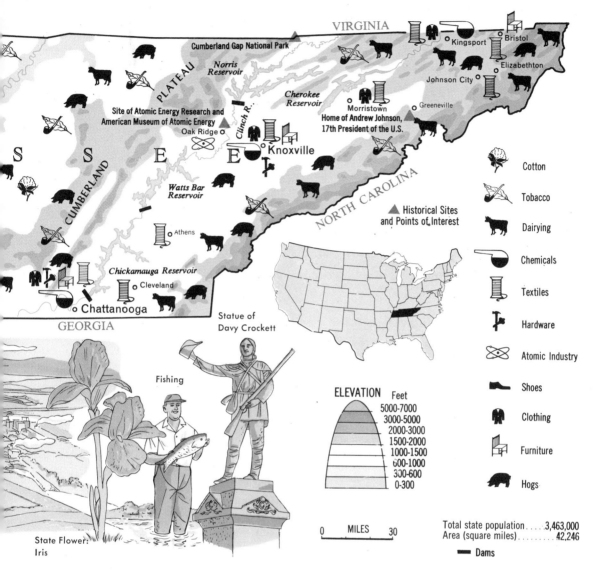

ELEVATION Feet
5000-7000
3000-5000
2000-3000
1500-2000
1000-1500
600-1000
300-600
0-300

0   MILES   30

Cotton
Tobacco
Dairying
Chemicals
Textiles
Hardware
Atomic Industry
Shoes
Clothing
Furniture
Hogs

Historical Sites
and Points of Interest

Fishing

State Flower:
Iris

Statue of
Davy Crockett

Total state population.....3,463,000
Area (square miles).........42,246
— Dams

"The West" slopes gently toward the Mississippi River. On the fertile lands near the river, farmers raise much cotton. Memphis ships many bales of cotton down the Mississippi River.

Today, industry brings more money to the people of Tennessee than farming. Factories are sure of plentiful electric power and coal, and of a variety of raw materials from farms, mines, and forests. The chemical industry leads all others. Among its chief products are rayon and nylon yarns, and cellophane. Other industries produce cloth, clothing, dairy products, and furniture. One of the world's largest aluminum plants is at Alcoa.

Both farming and manufacturing have been helped by the work of the TVA (Tennessee Valley Authority), created by the national government in 1933. World-famous dams and power plants were built to prevent flood damage, furnish electricity, improve navigation, and provide for recreation. These improvements have helped to bring great changes to eastern Tennessee. In 1942, Oak Ridge, Tennessee, became the first atomic energy center. Knoxville and Chattanooga are the two large cities in this rapidly growing industrial area. Memphis, the largest city in the state, is a thriving industrial center and Mississippi port. Tennessee is part of the "changed South."

TENNIS A great many different games are played with a ball. Tennis is one of them. A tennis ball is an air-filled rubber ball covered with flannel. It is made so that it bounces very well. The ball is hit with a racket back and forth across a net three feet high. A tennis racket is a frame with strands of catgut, silk, or nylon stretched across it. The frame is usually made of ash or hickory wood.

The game of tennis is very much like Ping-pong. Ping-pong, in fact, is often called table tennis.

To anyone who does not know the game, the score at times sounds strange. "Love" is used for "zero." If the score in a game is "15-love," one side has 15 points and the other side nothing. A game tied at 40-40 is a "deuce" game.

Tennis may be played by either two people or four. Games in which two people play are called "singles." "Doubles" are games with four players. Both men and women play tennis. If each team in a match is made up of a man and a woman, the match is called "mixed doubles."

"Tennis" is short for "lawn tennis." At first the game was played on grass-covered courts. But now many courts are bare. Some are clay-covered, some are concrete, and some are even covered with cinders.

The first tennis game ever played in the United States was played in 1874. Tennis had been invented only the year before by an English major. He called it by the peculiar name of "Sphairistike." No one liked the name, but many liked the game. Now tennis is played all over the world.

Although outdoor tennis is less than 100 years old, its ancestor—court tennis—goes back to the Middle Ages. Kings and noblemen played court tennis indoors in special rooms built for it.

Every year there are championship tennis matches. The two best-known trophies are the Davis Cup for men and the Wightman Cup for women. The Davis Cup

Backhand Return

Follow-through

Toss Up, Flat Serve

Forehand Return

A Volley

matches are international. The Wightman Cup matches are between American and British players. Other famous matches are those held at Wimbledon (England) and the matches for the United States national championships. Both men and women take part in these tournaments.

There are officials at tennis tournaments. But the players themselves help with the rulings. If a player makes a mistake which the official fails to see, the player reports it. No player accepts a point unless he is sure he is entitled to it. For this reason tennis is often called a "gentleman's game." (See GAMES AND SPORTS.)

TERMITES Long, long before people had cities some kinds of insects began living in groups and working together. Among these insects are the termites. Termite nests in the tropics are sometimes three times as tall as a man. But in cooler regions termite nests are hidden in wood or in the ground.

Termites eat almost nothing but wood. They eat away the inside of the legs of tables, chairs, and other pieces of furniture, making them unsafe to use. Whole houses fall down because termites have eaten away the inside of beams.

A termite "city" is made up of a king, a queen, and thousands or even millions of workers and soldiers. Young kings and queens have wings. After a marriage flight a king and a queen find a place for a nest. Then they lose their wings. The queen settles down to a life of laying eggs. She may lay 8,000 eggs a day for several years.

The workers and soldiers are wingless. The workers build the nests bigger and gather food. They feed and care for the queen, too. The soldiers have large heads and strong jaws. They protect the colony.

Termites are often wrongly called white ants. In one way they are very different from ants. They do not go through four stages as they grow up as ants do. Newly hatched termites look much like grown-up termites. They shed their hard outside covering from time to time as they get older and bigger.

There are several kinds of termites. Most termites never go far above the ground to reach dead wood. But some live in dry wood and never go near the ground. (See ANTS; INSECT PESTS.)

TEXAS When Alaska became the 49th state of the United States, Texas lost its first place in size among the states. But Texas can still boast of several first places.

Texas ranks first in value of mineral production. No other state produces anywhere near the over-a-billion barrels of crude petroleum pumped in one year from Texas oil fields. In fact, the state produces almost half the oil produced in the United States. Texas also leads the nation in natural gas, helium, and sulfur.

Texas leads all states in the number of farms and acres farmed. More cotton is grown on Texas farms than in any other state. Its ranches produce more cattle, sheep, and wool. Some of the cattle are white-faced Herefords; some are a cross-breed of shorthorn and Brahman. The famous King Ranch of more than a million acres is in Texas.

Texas is a prosperous state, but it is not crowded. Even though it ranks sixth in population among the states, there are fewer people in Texas than in New York City. There could be two or three times as many people without overcrowding.

Only about one-third of the Texans live on farms or in very small towns. But the farms produce, in addition to cotton, a variety of crops. Along the hot, wet Gulf Coast rice is one of the special crops. Along the lower Rio Grande there is an irrigated farming section. Texans here produce grapefruit and other citrus fruits, and vegetables for winter markets. The United States and Mexico together built the great Falcón Dam to control the flow of the lower Rio Grande. The dam supplies irrigation water to the dry land near by. It protects the farmland from floods and helps to run electric power plants. In north and northwest Texas there are huge wheat farms. Other crops are oats, barley, corn, rye, fruits, and nuts.

Almost two-thirds of all Texans live in cities. There are seven cities of more than 100,000 people. Houston, near the Gulf,

State Flag

Oil Derricks

The Alamo

Cowboy

El Paso
Picturesque Mexican Border City Dating Back to the Days of the Spanish Conquistadores

State Bird: Mockingbird

Oil

Sulphur

Textiles

Chemicals

Hardware

Machinery

Natural Gas

Helium

Beef Cattle

Cotton

Wheat

Meat Packing

Citrus Fruit

Sheep

Garden Crops

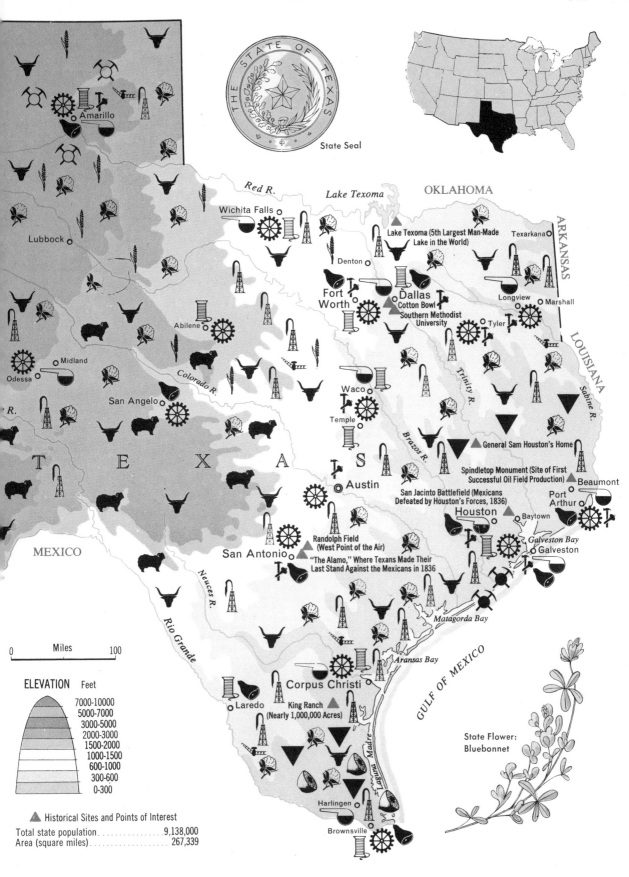

State Seal

Red R.

Lake Texoma

OKLAHOMA

ARKANSAS

Wichita Falls

Lake Texoma (5th Largest Man-Made Lake in the World)

Texarkana

Lubbock

Denton

Fort Worth

Dallas

Cotton Bowl
Southern Methodist University

Longview
Marshall

Amarillo

LOUISIANA

Abilene

Tyler

Midland

Colorado R.

Trinity R.

Sabine R.

Odessa

San Angelo

Waco

Temple

Brazos R.

General Sam Houston's Home

R.

T   E   X   A   S

Spindletop Monument (Site of First Successful Oil Field Production)

Beaumont

Austin

San Jacinto Battlefield (Mexicans Defeated by Houston's Forces, 1836)

Port Arthur

Houston

Baytown

Randolph Field (West Point of the Air)

Galveston Bay
Galveston

MEXICO

San Antonio

"The Alamo," Where Texans Made Their Last Stand Against the Mexicans in 1836

Neces R.

Matagorda Bay

Miles
0   100

Aransas Bay

GULF OF MEXICO

Rio Grande

Corpus Christi

ELEVATION   Feet

Laredo

King Ranch (Nearly 1,000,000 Acres)

7000-10000
5000-7000
3000-5000
2000-3000
1500-2000
1000-1500
600-1000
300-600
0-300

State Flower: Bluebonnet

Laguna Madre

Harlingen

▲ Historical Sites and Points of Interest
Total state population 9,138,000
Area (square miles) 267,339

Brownsville

has huge petroleum refineries, chemical plants, cottonseed oil mills, and flour mills. Corpus Christi, farther to the southwest, is another petroleum and trade center.

. Dallas is the biggest city in the cotton and oil region of northeastern Texas. Cotton is bought and sold at Dallas markets. Its factories manufacture textiles, cottonseed oil, and women's and children's clothing. Dallas has become well known as a fashion center. Hundreds of oil companies have their offices in Dallas. Fort Worth is a meat-packing center. Austin, the capital, is another manufacturing and trade center.

San Antonio is like these other cities in that it is a trade center. It differs, however, in that it has been a leading city since pioneer days and has many reminders of the early history of "The Lone Star State."

Texas was under Spanish or Mexican flags until 1836, when Texas declared its independence. The Alamo in San Antonio is a reminder of the Texans' heroic struggle for freedom. They finally won their freedom under their great leader, Sam Houston, and formed a republic. The Texas Republic had a flag with one star. In 1845 Texas was admitted to the Union. It flew the Confederate flag in the War between the States. This state that has been under four other flags is proud now to be under the flag of the United States.

Off in the farthest west corner of Texas is its seventh large city, El Paso. This city stands where the Rio Grande cuts through the mountains. It is thus a gateway to the West. El Paso is farther from Beaumont near the eastern boundary of Texas than Chicago is from New York. Texas is, indeed, a big sprawling state.

TEXTILES The word "textile" comes from a Latin word meaning "to weave." The word "textiles" refers to all kinds of cloth made by weaving.

For weaving there must be fibers of some kind. Up until the 20th century four fibers were much more important in making textiles than any others. They were cotton, linen, silk, and wool. Cotton and linen come from plants. Silk and wool are animal fibers. Today many of our textiles are made from man-made fibers. Rayon and nylon are two of the best known. New man-made fibers are being invented fast.

Almost all weaving is done on looms. For thousands of years the only looms were hand looms. Most of the weaving was done in homes. Now most weaving is done in mills, or factories, on looms driven by steam or electricity.

The United States has many textile mills. In a year those mills use about 8 million bales of cotton, 370 million pounds of wool, and 400 million pounds of rayon. They use millions of pounds of nylon, linen, and other fibers besides. About a million American workers earn their living in textile mills. (See COTTON; FIBERS; LINEN; NYLON; RAYON; SILK; SPINNING AND WEAVING; WOOL.)

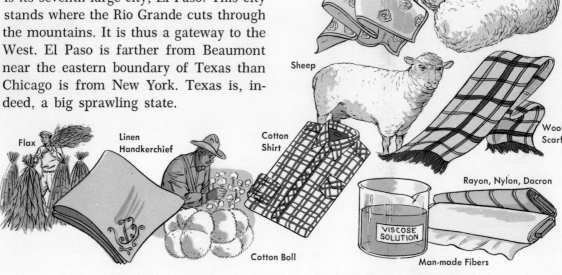

Silk Material   Silkworm Cocoon

Sheep

Wool Scarf

Flax   Linen Handkerchief   Cotton Shirt

Rayon, Nylon, Dacron

VISCOSE SOLUTION

Cotton Boll   Man-made Fibers